Teaching Language ~~r~~ ~~cy~~ in the Early Years

Diane Godwin and Margaret Perkins

David Fulton Publishers
London

372.
6
GOD

David Fulton Publishers Ltd
Ormond House, 26–27 Boswell Street, London WC1N 3JD

First published in Great Britain by David Fulton Publishers 1998
Reprinted 1999

British Library Cataloguing in Publication Data
A catalogue record for this book is available from the British Library

ISBN 1–85346–529–1

Typeset by FSH Print and Production Ltd, London
Printed in Great Britain by Cromwell Press Ltd, Trowbridge, Wilts.

Contents

For Alan
and
For Ben

Acknowledgements

We are grateful to the teachers, students and children who over the years have provided us with the joy of sharing in their teaching and learning. Many of the examples used in this book come from them and we wish to acknowledge our debt to them. We are particularly grateful to St Clement's CE Primary School, Worcester, where many of the photographs were taken.

In case of failure to obtain permission to include copyright material in this book, the authors and publishers apologise and undertake to make good omissions in subsequent printings.

Introduction

Why this book?

This book was written as an attempt to point the way to good practice in early years work. The teaching of language and literacy is one which hits the headlines and we wanted to help students and other adults working with young children to access easily the relevant research and to see what that research means in practical terms in an early years setting. This book makes no claims to full coverage of all the areas; it acts as an introduction and at times indicates possibilities of further reading and reflection.

Who is this book for?

This book is written specifically for those who are preparing to work in an early years setting and want to know how to implement the requirements of the Desirable Outcomes (SCAA 1996) with particular reference to language and literacy. It is also for those who may have been working with young children for some time and want to find out what current thinking is on language and literacy teaching and learning. It is also for anyone who loves young children, who loves observing them as they begin to make sense of the world around them and wishes to know more of the processes that are going on.

There are a variety of contexts in which very young children begin their education and the terminology used in the book reflects that variety. We talk about classrooms, settings and nurseries; we mention teachers and adults. In all cases what we say can be applied in any context.

What will this book do?

It is hoped that in this book we have shown that theory and research have a direct impact on practice and that effective practice comes from a knowledge and understanding of relevant research. We believe strongly in the notion of the 'reflective practitioner' as one who is continually seeking to improve practice. Those working with young children must not be mere technicians but must have a firm understanding of the ways in which young children learn and the ways in which we can best teach them.

Who wrote this book?

This book is written by two people who between them have many years of experience of working with young children in playgroups, private nurseries, nursery classes and reception classes. We have both taught students preparing to be early years teachers and have worked with teachers who wished to improve their practice. We both have a passion for the importance of language and literacy, believing that language is central to the learning process, that young children come into the early years setting as experienced learners with a lot of expertise in language and that it is our responsibility to make that knowledge explicit and to extend and develop it in order to empower children to be critical and reflective citizens of the future. Above all, this book arises from our love of young children, our joy in being with them, observing them, talking and playing with them and learning from them.

In what context was this book written?

As we write this, talk in the media and in government is of falling standards in literacy and strategies are being adopted to raise those standards. The government is preparing to launch its Literacy Initiative (1997–2002) and 1998/99 has been declared the 'Year of Reading'. Targets are being set and local authorities and individual schools are required to set their own targets and show how they plan to achieve them.

The National Literacy Project (1996) has been a strong influence on this movement. It offers a framework of clear learning outcomes broken down in great detail for each term from reception through to Year 6, outlining work to be covered at text, sentence and word level. Just one example of these outcomes is that during Year 1 pupils are required to become familiar with and use the term phoneme. The National Literacy Project advocates the literacy hour; sixty minutes of fast-paced explicit focused literacy teaching. There is a high proportion of whole-class work and the teacher is engaged in direct instruction for every minute of that hour. From September 1998 schools are required to implement the literacy hour or demonstrate that their chosen teaching method is as effective in raising standards. It is not expected that nursery classes will engage in this but certainly one can expect to see reception classes having a literacy hour.

It is in this context of an increased expectation of direct instruction and more whole-class work that the age range of many nursery and reception classes has changed. The introduction of the nursery voucher scheme in 1996, meant that settings containing four-year-olds were required to register and be open to inspection. This resulted in many schools taking younger children into their reception classes in order to take advantage of the vouchers and, despite the abandonment of the voucher scheme, the situation remains where some children enter the reception year in the September of the year in which they are 5. Some of these children are only just 4 and so it is vital that the learning opportunities and resources provided are appropriate for them. Those working in early years settings need to resist the pressure to embark on the curriculum for Key Stage 1 before the children are intellectually and emotionally ready.

Alongside all this is the development of baseline assessment. From 1998 it is a statutory requirement for local education authorities to have a baseline assessment scheme in place. The assessments will be made when children are getting used to a new setting and a new social group and so it is important that the form of assessment allows children to show what they can do, understand and know and so needs to take place over a period of time. The Association of Assessment Inspectors and Advisers (1997) identifies one of the purposes of a baseline scheme as being to 'support the introduction of children to the National Curriculum Programmes of Study, as and when appropriate'. Early years practitioners must resist any pressure to modify the curriculum to introduce inappropriate activities too soon. It is hoped that this book will show that effective teaching and learning can take place within a setting where the children's existing knowledge is valued and play is at the centre of the curriculum.

How is this book structured?

Most of the chapters are written to the same structure. The first section briefly defines terms and introduces the relevant parts of the Desirable Outcomes. Secondly we look at what children actually do; observation is one of the most important skills an adult working in the early years can possess and we want to stress that our starting point is always the children and their naturally observed behaviours. We then go on in the third section to look at what research can tell us, using research evidence to explain and question what the children do.

The next three sections help the practitioner to take these understandings and relate them to practice. We look at play, focused activities and the environment. In each of these sections we outline some practical things that can be done in most settings.

The seventh section considers the planning, assessing, recording and reporting cycle and each chapter looks at a different aspect to build up skills and understanding.

The final chapter does not follow the structure of the others and serves as a drawing together of all that has been said beforehand – hence its title, 'Play: Making the Whole'. It is about play and the importance we give to play is because we see it as underpinning and fulfilling all that has gone before. It has been said many times before, but is worth repeating, that play is the work of the young child and as such should hold a dominant position within any early years setting, as it does in this book.

1: Talk

1.1 Defining terms

This chapter has been written with a view to placing language development firmly in the context of social and cognitive development. The Desirable Outcomes state that language development is marked by the ability to 'use a growing vocabulary with increasing fluency to express thoughts and convey meaning to the listener'. A feature of good practice is where 'approaches to teaching include recognition of the value of providing first hand experiences ... and of using play and talk as media for learning'.

These statements form the foundation for discussion as we look at children's development as language users where talk is seen as an act of meaningful communication and the company the child keeps is fundamental to his/her learning. We look at the pattern of the early development of talk and the factors which affect this development.

1.2 What children do

You will see from section 1.1 that the second desirable outcome we refer to comes from the section entitled 'Common Features of Good Practice'. Look through this document and you will see from the many references that situations which invite children to talk will present themselves across the early years curriculum. These references are indicative of the importance of language development in the early years.

We are going to organise our discussion of language development using 'express thoughts and convey meaning' and 'talk as a medium for learning' as a framework.

Using language to express thoughts and convey meaning

This sets language firmly in the context of social interaction where communication is paramount. Language development is 'helped by unconscious invitation, it is stimulated by the response of others and speech becomes clearer in the necessity for communication' (Wilkinson 1965).

The term 'Oracy', used to denote speaking and listening, was coined by Andrew Wilkinson in 1965, and we introduce you to it here as it is used widely in educational environments where practitioners are keen to promote the status of speaking and listening to that attained by reading and writing. He provided this model which introduces two dimensions of language, the production and the reception:

	PRODUCTION	RECEPTION
ORACY	SPEAKING	LISTENING
LITERACY	WRITING	READING

This gives us an interesting alternative to the way we are used to categorising language in education. The National Curriculum defines the aspects of English as speaking and listening, and reading and writing. This divides the English curriculum into two parts, oracy and literacy. Had the authors of the National Curriculum chosen to follow a production/reception divide we would have aspects entitled speaking and writing, and listening and reading. There is an attraction to this in that it brings to the fore the similarities between oral and written communication. Think about this for a while; how many similarities can you find between speaking and writing, and listening and reading? Perhaps you said that both speaking and writing are about communicating to an audience and both require awareness of the needs of the audience, to have their attention engaged for example. Most children know implicitly that they must gain the attention of those they wish to talk to and this knowledge can be a powerful support in their learning about writing. Similarly, most children know that there are occasions when they must attend carefully to what is being said to them. The knowledge that the child has accumulated in learning to talk will provide him/her with a powerful support when learning to read.

Have you ever thought about what it is you do when you are talking? Ingram (1993) considers the analysis of a conversation between friends over lunch. You and your partner know how to take turns, but there is much more to it than that.

- Did you know that you give signals to indicate when it is your friend's turn to take over the conversation and that s/he does the same so that you rarely speak over one another?
- Did you know that, if you don't want to speak, you might 'back channel'; you say simply 'yeah' or 'ah' in exactly the space your partner has left for you and give the conversational ball back to him/her?
- Did you know that if you want to move the conversation on you might 'override' your partner by speaking the same words in parallel, thereby bringing the subject to a close or indicating that you know that bit?
- Did you know that, if you need time to think about what you are going to say next you will avert your gaze, and when you are ready you will gaze at your partner?

Ingram mentions many more similar cues which we use effortlessly but which, when analysed, reveal the complexity of the conversational interchange. 'It took two years to analyse forty minutes of conversation, and ... of 264 smooth exchanges in the conversations (they) analysed, 261 were preceded by one or more of these signals'. The point being made here is that we all learn to make and respond to these signals without any explicit instruction. So, how do we know that? What is it that makes us able to do it? What would you say in answer to the question, how did you learn to talk?

Your reply will almost certainly make reference to other people, your social environment, significant people who welcomed you into their speaking world. But what did they do that encouraged you to join in?

Perhaps it went something like this:

- You were born into a family where relationships were established and where the members of the group shared many experiences such as shopping together, watching television, celebrating birthdays. This shared context meant that your parents, siblings, and other close friends and relatives were able to treat you on more or less equal terms regarding the topic and style of communication, and then to encourage you to greater competence.
- You were not always included directly, of course, but when you were, your conversational partner will have modified his/her own speech to make sure that

you each were following what the other was saying. At other times you will simply have heard others talking between themselves in a variety of different ways, e.g. arguing, questioning, planning, discussing, explaining. In this way you, the learner, received many models of talk.

- From the moment you started to take interest in the world you will have begun to realise that talk is important; everybody was doing it, everybody was using it to communicate and build relationships.

So, your family and friends gave you reasons to talk and many examples of talk, but you were not just the recipient of their efforts. You soon learned that your very first sounds could get things done, could direct others, could communicate pleasure or discomfort. From then you quickly learned to deploy and develop your linguistic skills, and to this day you continue to develop as a speaker and listener in a variety of different communities that accept you as a participant, and where social interaction is fundamental to your continuing growth as a language user.

The story could be different. We could identify factors which might discourage and inhibit talk. We feel less able to talk when:

- other people ridicule the way we talk, maybe by laughing at our accent or dialect;
- we don't know the other members of the group we are in, or we think they know more than we do;
- it is clear the other person is not listening, or has no interest in what we are saying;
- we are shy.

There are many reasons why we might choose not to talk, and that is a valid choice of course. But how many times have you wanted to take part yet been silenced by any of the above? Many of my students nod in agreement when I recall my own frustration at school, when the teacher asked a question and I was too nervous to answer even though I was right. I suppose I was afraid I might make a mistake, perhaps I thought others would laugh at me, perhaps I lacked confidence.

Factors which support language learning

Confidence is a key factor in children's language and learning development. Barrs *et al.* (1990) put forward 'five dimensions of learning' that help us to be more discriminating when we are observing language and learning. The authors point out that they are inter-connected and support each other, and although the publication was written with the English National Curriculum Key Stages 1 and 2 in mind, it has much to say about language learning in general. We refer to it here because the five dimensions (confidence and independence; experience; strategies; knowledge and understanding; and reflectiveness) can all be traced through the Desirable Outcomes. For example:

Confidence and independence
'Children are confident, show appropriate self-respect and are able to establish effective relationships with other children and adults' (p. 2).

Experience
'Children talk about where they live, their environment, their families and past and present events in their own lives' (p. 4).

Strategies

'Eager to explore new learning, and show the ability to initiate ideas and to solve simple practical problems' (p. 2). 'They use a widening range of materials, suitable tools, instruments and other resources to express ideas and to communicate feelings' (p. 4).

Reflectiveness

'Children are encouraged to think and talk about their learning and to develop self-control and independence' (p. 6).

The Desirable Outcomes in their entirety are examples of children's growing knowledge and understanding. Language development is influenced by all of the above and therefore, when planning for or assessing children's language development we should give them careful consideration. We may think, for example, that we have set up an opportunity for a child to 'express thoughts to the listener' but if the child lacks confidence then it is possible that the outcomes reflect this rather than his/her ability as language user. Language development does not happen in isolation. It happens when the climate in which the child operates is supportive to the child. For example, when:

- feeling confident with the people s/he is talking with;
- having a rich background of experiences which s/he can share with others;
- actively and enthusiastically exploring and experimenting with new ideas, and using the expertise and contributions of others;
- being able to talk with others about his/her world and what s/he thinks and feels about it;
- being invited by others to look back on an event or experience and to learn from it.

We have chosen to describe here aspects of the learning environment which emphasise the social nature of language learning. Other people matter; the people the child talks to will have an effect on the child's own language and learning. The adult in the early years setting has significant effect and therefore considerable responsibility: part of this responsibility is to convey to the children that talking and listening are the most important ways of communicating and that they are powerful instruments for learning.

Multilingual children

Before children enter the early years setting they will already be able to communicate and learn through language, although the language they use will not necessarily be English. One of my most significant learning experiences was following a discussion with a five-year-old boy in a North London school. He told me that he could talk in seven languages and read and write a little in two. I was particularly impressed by the way in which he could compare and contrast his several languages. He could talk about talk as if he could see it, and I knew that this ability was significant in language awareness. His multilingualism was a positive support to knowing about language.

How do you feel about children who have a different way of talking? Perhaps a different accent, dialect or language? Did you know that 70 per cent of the world's population are bi- or multi-lingual? Inevitably many of the children we work with will be learning in more than one language, so how can we provide experiences which enable them to use what they know, and which reflect the multi-lingual society in which we live? We can begin by:

- encouraging children to talk in their preferred language when they find it gives greater support to effective communication and learning. Children whose first language is not English already have considerable knowledge of one language system which they can transfer and use in the mastery of English. 'Children must be helped to acquire competence in English as soon as possible, making use, where appropriate, of their developing skills and understanding in other languages' (*Desirable Outcomes*, p. 3). They have also developed strategies for learning in one language which may well serve them better in certain situations. Multilingual children are not children with learning difficulties;
- inviting people who share the child's language into the setting. In this way children will be encouraged to continue developing competence in their home language as well as English, thereby retaining their multilingualism;
- valuing their language and their culture by providing resources, displays and activities which reflect their experiences and histories.

The Primary Language Record was recommended to the National Curriculum Council as a model for the assessment of children's development as language users and we recommend it to you here. The authors embrace languages other than English and give us an insight into the needs of learners of English as a second language: 'In learning to use a second language children generally move through development phases that mirror those they moved through in learning a first language' (Barrs *et al*. 1988, p. 20).

Phases of language development

Most texts dealing with child development describe the first five years of a child's life as one of rapid learning where children learn to master the complexities of talking in an environment of support and sharing. There is a clear pattern to the child's language development in any language, and it can be described briefly as follows.

In the child's first year s/he produces sounds such as cooing and grunting. This babble becomes strings of sounds with intonation. If you have ever heard a child 'conversing' this way you will probably have been surprised and delighted at the strength of his/her commitment to what is being 'said'. If the child is a stranger to you then you are unlikely to understand what s/he means because the words are not recognisable, they are pre-communicative. Should you know the child, however, you may well be able to interpret his/her utterances and respond appropriately. Knowing the child and the context make it possible to have meaningful exchanges using his/her individual form of language. You may find it interesting to know that some call this pre-communicative talk 'jargon'; it is a special language understood by the members of a close community.

Usually, in the child's second year the first 'words' appear, although they may still be unrecognisable to the wider audience; however, those closer to the child begin to see that the child uses them consistently and regularly to represent the same or similar meanings and can confidently interpret on the child's behalf. The same adult can also initiate another into the child's language use. Sometimes the adult will respond using the child's actual words and other times the adult will feed back the conventional words thereby modelling correct forms for the child to adopt. In many interactions, where adult and child negotiate meanings, the child enters a transition phase where his/her conventional spoken vocabulary grows from around 20 words at 18 months to 200 words at 21 months. Your mathematics will tell you that this is a growth rate of approximately 15 words each week. This rapid rate of acquisition accelerates to around 10 new words a day until the child of 3 has a vocabulary of 1,000 words, and at 5 has around 5,000 words.

When a child has a vocabulary of only a few words then the possibility of joining these words together exists. At around 18 months the child begins to utter simple sentences and demonstrates another rapid growth in his/her linguistic abilities. In putting words together in the correct order the child's awareness of grammar develops, and by 3 years of age s/he will be producing many three or four word sentences. At this point most adults and other children find they can understand and conversation becomes more conventional. 'By the age of 5 children from all cultures understand and use most of the grammatical rules of their language, communicate effectively with peers and adults and demonstrate inventive ways of expressing themselves with words' (Smith and Cowie 1988, p. 241).

We have used the adjectives pre-communicative, transitional and conventional because we want to establish the links between oracy and literacy. Later, we will use them again in relation to children's early writing, which exhibits a similar pattern of development.

Using talk as a medium for learning

Just as oracy and literacy are dependent on one another, so too are linguistic and cognitive development. Vygotsky (1962) suggested that 'speech in infancy is the direct antecedent of thinking at a later stage'. When children engage in conversation they are developing their knowledge of grammar and extending their vocabulary, but when they talk to and for themselves (from 3 to 7 years of age),

> speech takes on a dual function and, in due course, develops differentially; conversation becomes more effective as communication, while monologue or 'running commentary' (speech for oneself) changes in what is virtually the opposite direction ... speech for oneself became internalised and continued to operate as the genesis of thought, perhaps moving through the stages of inner speech to verbal thinking and thence to the most elusive stage of all – thought itself (Brindley 1994, p. 261).

Have you ever seen a child making such a running commentary? If you have worked or lived with young children you must have seen many examples of this. But you may not have connected this with thinking or conceptual development. We will return to Vygotsky's work later. In the meantime we hope this gives you a taste of the theoretical thinking which makes the link between language and thought, and that you can see how the vocabulary and grammar acquired during conversation can feed and enhance the monologue children employ when they are 'talking to themselves' or pre-thinking.

Conceptual development, with language, begins when the child starts to interact with the world and the people in it. From the moment a child is born the adults around begin to induct him/her into the social community s/he has joined. The adult smiles, tickles, tut-tuts, scolds, laughs, talks, sings, frowns and the child touches, tastes, smells, gasps, cries, smiles, jiggles, writhes and laughs, in a complex process of learning about the way things go 'around here'. Ask any parent and they will tell you that the child is not a passive recipient in this process. The baby initiates and controls many of these interchanges. The entire context in which the child operates influences and affects the child's development as language user and learner. This being the case

> if speech in childhood lays the foundation for a lifetime of thinking, how can we continue to prize a silent classroom? And if shared social behaviour is seen as the source of learning, we must revise the traditional view of the teacher's role. The teacher can no longer act as the 'middle-man' in all learning – as it becomes clear that education is an effect of community. (Brindley 1994, p. 262).

The community described in this book reflects this interplay between linguistic, social and cognitive development where the members of that community, children and adults, are active in the learning process. The next section will look at theories of learning and the role of the teacher in providing an environment for language and learning.

1.3 What the research says

Many have tried to explain what is actually happening as a child develops linguistically and how it comes about that s/he is able to master such a complex set of procedures with relative ease. Tann (1991) describes four main alternative models put forward to explain how children acquire language.

Imitative, behaviourist theories propounded by B. S. Skinner are based on the notion that children learn by copying what they hear around them. We can all find examples of children copying adults and a theory which suggests that language is acquired by imitation is attractive in its simplicity. But the rate at which children expand their vocabulary suggests that something more happens than simply hearing a word and memorising it.

Chomsky suggested that human beings are born with a language acquisition device, a kind of blueprint that is triggered by the language they hear around them. Chomsky recognised that children create words and sentences they have never heard before, linguistically they give out more than we put in. The idea that children are pre-programmed to generate language can lead to the minimalisation of the roles of the environment and the adult in children's learning.

Interaction theories are associated with Bruner who suggested that it is the interaction between the adult and the child that counts and that the nature of the language environment supports the child's efforts to learn. The environment is the focal point for those who see learning as an individual endeavour, that is, that the child takes from his/her environment what s/he needs to further understanding. The adult's role here is to provide a supportive, interactive environment and only intervene when the child needs support in reaching that understanding.

In the cultural-communicative approach the emphasis is on negotiated meanings and the importance of surrounding contexts which enhance the interaction between adult and child. The interplay between the child, the environment and the adult, helps the child move on in their implicit knowledge about language. The adult can 'lend' what they know, understand and can do to children. They can do this to take the child into the next progressive step in their learning, their Zone of Proximal Development (ZPD) as Vygotsky terms it. You may have heard the phrase 'what the child can do today with help, he can do tomorrow on his own'.

Theories of learning, or cognitive development, can be readily accessed in publications associated with child development. Most will refer to Piaget, and Meadows (1992) provides us with a helpful insight, including the challenges, into his work. Despite these challenges and criticisms two features of his philosophy remain key to early childhood education. The first is that children are active in their attempts to make sense of the world and their place within it. The second is that learning requires the assimilation and accommodation of new knowledge to old. Various models of learning have grown from Piaget's and others' theories of learning, and we want to introduce you to that generated by Reid, Forrestal and Cook (1989). This model has since been widely used by teachers to promote talk in their classrooms. We feel it has a useful application for the early years setting and reproduce it here so that you can use it as you plan for learning in your own environment. The model suggests this sequence of learning:

Sequence of learning

Engagement (setting the scene)
'... intention to learn is aroused, when they (children) become curious or puzzled about what they are to learn ... What they learn must, therefore, matter to them as well as to their teacher' (Howe and Johnson 1992, p. 159).

Exploration
' ... allowed pupils to become involved in the learning process by relating new information to their past experiences' (Howe and Johnson 1992, p. 161).

Transformation
This is a play stage where new information is re-shaped and worked with so that the learner can move closer to further understanding.

Presentation
' ... strategies whereby the learners explain their developing understandings to others play an important part in the process of assimilating new information' (Howe and Johnson 1992, p. 163).

Reflection
Reflection on what and how they have learned is an important part in accommodating new information into what they already know.

Consider this model in relation to your own learning. What have you recently learned? To drive a car perhaps? You must have had a clear reason to want to learn to drive: it mattered to you (engagement). As a passenger you previously watched another driver and wondered how well you would steer, brake, consider other drivers, etc.

(exploration of your own potential). When you were behind the wheel at first, it probably was rather more difficult than you imagined. Perhaps your gear changes weren't as smooth as you would have liked! (transformation to competent driver). Finally your test, and your chance to demonstrate what you have learned (presentation). You passed! Now you want to tell everybody about it, how nervous you were, how you nearly went up on to the pavement when reversing round a corner, how you are going to do things differently from now on (reflection). Of course it wasn't exactly like this, but can you see how these stages can help you plan learning opportunities for children?

'The model was intended to provide a structure to help teachers to plan rather than as a strict formula which needs to be followed rigidly' (p. 165) Consider, for example, the common practice of reading a story to children. What can be done to engage their interest? Perhaps use a picture or an object and ask them to offer their reactions to it, drawing out what they already know about it, exploring it in relation to their own experiences. When you read the story you could invite the children to anticipate what might happen next, giving them the opportunity to transform what they hear and see in order to understand more clearly the type of story or what is happening in it. No doubt you will give them the chance to explain their reactions to the story and/or pictures, to present their thinking to others. A short discussion at the end of the story will help them reflect on their responses, their interpretations, their expectations, etc.

The model is flexible, and you won't proceed in as orderly a way as this, nor will you do this every time, as that would result in boredom and predictability. However, you should reflect on the activities that you provide for children to make sure that they do receive opportunities to reflect, etc.

The influence of Piaget's philosophy regarding active learning and the process outlined above can be seen in an approach to the early years curriculum called High Scope (Hohman *et al.* 1979). The plan–do–review cycle within this approach mirrors the developmental learning model outlined here. Children in a nursery following the High Scope approach find themselves in a daily routine aimed at giving the children the opportunity to make choices and be independent learners. The children signal their intentions to an adult who helps them articulate their 'plan' and is able to support them in their learning during later activity. When the children have finished planning (and this might be simply fetching a toy they want to play with) they move to the work time where they 'do'. Here the adult first observes and then intervenes to encourage and extend the child's learning. The final activity is where the child describes what they have done and 'reviews' how their plans went.

The Desirable Outcomes in 'Common Features of Good Practice' 'do not prescribe a particular or preferred curriculum or teaching approach' (p. 6). However, they do identify the following as 'a helpful context when planning the curriculum':

- children feeling secure, valued and confident;
- children participating in a range of activities which take due account of their interests;
- children being encouraged to think and talk about their learning;
- children being encouraged to develop self-control and independence;
- approaches to teaching including recognition of the value of providing first hand experiences.

These could well provide a checklist for evaluating your own setting, and for researching other approaches like Steiner or Montessori.

1.4 Key concepts

In this first chapter our focus has been on oracy, or speaking and listening. We have introduced the concept that oracy and literacy are interrelated and that early language acquisition is developmental with certain recognisable features. Children learn to talk in a social climate where language is used both as a means of communication and as a tool for thought.

Donaldson (1978) asserts that language and learning cannot be separated from one another: 'it is the child's ability to interpret situations which make it possible for him, through the active process of hypothesis-testing and inference, to arrive at a knowledge of language' (p. 38). We recommend you read this short but thought-provoking text to further develop your own knowledge about language and learning.

Finally we will now offer you an explicit definition of the role of the adult in the early years setting. Until now this has been implied as we have described the wider needs of the learner (the five dimensions) and offered a model of learning which encompasses the principles of early language and learning.

The National Oracy Project published material relating to the role of the adult whose responsibility is to encourage and support talk (Norman 1992).

We have used their descriptions, enabler, modeller, sharer, and support, in order to reach a definition of the role of the adult in the context of our own writing.

The practitioner as enabler

The adult in the early years setting plans for talk and encourages talk for a variety of purposes and with a variety of talk partners, other adults and other children. S/he is aware of, and makes provision for, the needs of the learner to feel confident and independent in their own learning.

The practitioner as modeller

The adult in the early years setting communicates the status of talk to the children, parents and other interested parties by valuing talk as a process which helps children build relationships, as a tool for learning across the curriculum, and as a vehicle through which children can come to understand the many and varied experiences they have in and out of the setting. This is achieved by statement and by demonstration as the adult engages in conversation with children, actively listening and valuing their contributions.

The practitioner as sharer of roles

The adult in the early years setting involves the children in much of the planning and the activity of the setting, by using the children's own experiences and existing knowledge, encouraging children to question, and by consulting children on issues which involve them.

The practitioner as support

The adult in the early years setting offers his/her linguistic, social and cognitive awareness and skills to the children in order to help them move forward in their own knowledge, skills and understandings. S/he intervenes sensitively using his/her powers of observation to plan the next steps in the child's learning and to monitor the child's development. Much of this intervention will be spontaneous in response to the child's own thinking, picking up cues from the child.

1.5   Talk in play

Because talk pervades all areas of the early years curriculum, we recommend that you spend some time observing and reflecting on the activities provided. Sometimes the addition of a simple resource such as a telephone or a microphone can make all the difference in the quality of talk during play. We have compiled a list setting out the range of talk experiences which you should expect to observe as children play. Use this to reflect on your observations of children working with sand, water, dough, puzzles, dolls, cars, bricks, pencil and paper, paint, climbing frame, etc. The idea is to identify where and under what circumstances certain types of talk occur and then to consider ways in which they could be enriched. Of course children will talk in a range of ways in just one activity, but the process should enable you to identify any gaps in provision and take steps to modify it if necessary. The following talk audit (Figure 1.2) has been compiled directly from the Desirable Outcomes, with some additions.

Figure 1.1 Girl on telephone

1.6 Talk in focused activities

There will be times when you will plan specifically for talk within focused activities, i.e. activities which occur as part of a topic, which require the help of an adult, or

Range of talk opportunities provided in the setting	Where does this talk take place?	What can we do to enhance it?
• Listen attentively		
• Talk about their experiences and observations		
• Express thoughts		
• Convey meaning		
• Listen and respond to stories, songs, nursery rhymes and poems		
• Make up their own stories		
• Take part in role play		
• Use mathematical language e.g. circle, in front of		
• Talk about where they live, their environment, their families, past and present events in their own lives		
• Ask questions to gain information		

Figure 1.2 Talk audit

which are designed to introduce new concepts or skills. Here are some ideas which you could modify to suit your own purposes. We have included possible learning intentions (purposes) which relate directly to the ten types of talk offered in the talk audit in the previous section.

Taped story

Purpose
To give children experience of conveying meaning and expression in their storytelling.

Organisation
Designate a recording area which could be a small table and chair in a quiet corner. Provide a tape recorder and a blank cassette (a number of short cassettes are easier to manage than one long one as you need a strategy for identifying the speaker). Have one tape for each child in the small group. Placing the recorder on a square of carpeting or folded towel will help eliminate surrounding noise.

Give the children an overall purpose and audience for their story, e.g. a well-known fairy story for other children, a story about hamsters for the pet hamster, a story to cheer up a sad teddy. Remember to tell the children in advance what is going to happen to their story.

Ensure that the children have had time to play with the tape recorder and are able to operate the controls themselves. Many children will have had previous experience of recording at home and they can show other children.

Activities

Having ensured that the children know how to tape, that they have full understanding of the task and have the necessary resources, there are several ways the activity could proceed:

- The children tape a story and play it back to a known audience.
- The children tape a story and play it back to another (adult, child or whole group) for response and comment. Response should be positive and helpful, giving suggestions of ways it might be improved.
- The children tape more than one story and the group selects favourites, explaining why they prefer one over the other.
- The children tape a story and it is used as a voice-over for puppetry or drama presentation.
- The children tape a story and it is transcribed and illustrated for the book corner.

An interview

As above, ensure that the children know how to use the tape recorder. The children will also need an audience and a purpose for their interviewing. The purpose, given that the focus is on finding out, will always begin 'to find out'. Here are a range of possibilities:

- to find out what food, toys, games, television programmes, colours, clothes, pets, children like best;
- to find out how to make a lego house or how to play a favourite game.

Children can interview other children regarding the what, why, when and how of almost anything the other children are experienced in. The audience can extend to outside the setting, to family members and family friends, This gives access to a greater variety of experience over a wider expanse of time. Some children we know interviewed their grandparents to find out what games they played when they were children. Consider the implications of sending equipment home and prepare for these. It may be that a letter of explanation to the adults will be helpful.

Activity

A group of children and an adult discuss what it is they want to find out and how they may go about it. A flipchart is useful to brainstorm ideas and negotiate possible questions. Remember to edit the questions to a manageable number according to the children's ability to remember them. The children then carry out the interviews and the information retrieved by the children should be used. Again, as a small group working with an adult the children can tally and record on a chart the answer to the question or construct an information text.

There are more activities using a tape recorder throughout the book because any activity which captures talk for reflection and discussion will enhance the speaking and listening profile of the setting.

Finger puppets

Purpose
To give children the opportunity to make up their own stories.

Organisation
This requires few resources and lots of imagination. All you need are your and the children's fingers and a fine felt-tipped pen (the kind that washes off!). Find a willing volunteer and draw faces with various expressions on each finger (Fig. 1.3). Repeat on your own fingers. Talk about what the expressions mean.

Figure 1.3 Expressive faces

Begin a dialogue between the fingers, taking on happy and sad voices and explaining why it is that this finger looks happy and that one feels sad. Let your finger do the talking! Encourage the children to do the same among themselves. Eavesdrop on the various conversations, looking for stories which could be worked upon by a small group and turned into a book or acted out.

You do as I do

Purpose
The children will learn to give and receive directions paying attention to detail.

Organisation
You will need resources which allow a variety of situational possibilities. Bricks most obviously come to mind here, but almost anything will do where a number of alternative arrangements are possible. For example, you could use three model people and three model horses, provided each had a strong identifying feature. You will need two identical sets of whatever you choose to use. You will also need a screen which enables one child to create a pattern without the other seeing it. A large box on its side will do, then the describer can make the arrangement inside the box without the guesser seeing. The guesser then has to re-create the arrangement on the other side of the screen following the directions of the describer.

Children love this kind of guessing game and it can be played with a small group until the children get used to the rules and then the game can become part of the regular provision in the setting. Ideally the communication will be in words only, but for some children you may consider allowing gesture as well. Encourage team work; it is the describer's job to help the guesser make a similar model.

1.7 Talk in the environment

This section asks you to think about the kind of setting that you want to create for children: a setting which enables you to put into action all that you know about talk and children's development as speakers and listeners. There are three major factors in our experience which contribute to that which we would call an enriching environment for talk.

Contexts for talk

In such an environment we would see children playing, talking and working together in contexts which have been designed specifically to promote talk and provide children with meaningful purposes and real audiences for their talk.

Contexts for talk often arise from the children's own experiences and interests. It is a matter of being tuned in to what is going on in the community and what captivates children's imaginations. The adult who has a genuine interest in these things is advantaged because s/he will soon learn to pick up on local issues and themes which can be used to provide real, meaningful situations in which children can learn. Some examples to illustrate what is meant here are:

- the time when children were going to have their play area extended to include a 'natural' garden. The plans for the children included interviewing each other and neighbours about what should be included in the garden; brainstorming a shopping list of plants which attract insects and butterflies and then going shopping to buy them; planning the layout and, with the help of parents, digging and planting and finally making a set of rules about how the area should be used.
- the time when a mother shared her experience of looking after a baby and brought him into the nursery to bath and feed. All the children contributed to making a book about babies; they brought in photographs of themselves as babies and dictated their own personal stories; they talked to their parents in order to find out about themselves as babies; they discussed the way babies talk and they set up their own baby clinic where they were able to re-enact what they were learning.
- the time when the pet guinea pig had to visit the vet. The children made her get well cards and a special quiet area so she could rest; they talked about how it feels to be unwell and the kinds of things which help you to feel better; they wrote a letter to the vet thanking her for looking after their pet and this led to an exchange of letters and information.

These are just three contexts which we have experienced. We hope you can imagine the conversations, negotiations, plans, questions and explanations which would have arisen from the adults' intentions for and interactions with the children.

Raising the status of talk

Around the setting should be evidence of the resources and displays which celebrate talk. Here are just some of the things we have seen which show that talk has a high profile:

- tape recorders with blank and pre-recorded tapes for use by children and adults. Story tapes, taped sounds, children's own recordings;
- posters celebrating talk, e.g. 'the things mums/dads/brothers/sisters say', 'words we say when we are happy/angry/sad';
- talking wall: an area of wall covered in brick effect wallpaper so that when someone says something interesting/funny/helpful the adult can record it on a brick. The aim is to fill the wall with things we have heard somebody say;
- pictures on the wall with homemade speech bubbles and a variety of possible utterances;
- a story wall where pictures or photographs have been sequenced and the children have contributed captions;
- a talk chair. One teacher painted an old wooden child's chair bright yellow and used it as a story chair, the expert's chair, the nursery rhyme chair, the Goldilock's chair, etc.;
- the magic carpet which whisks you off to the land of make-believe;
- dressing-up clothes, jewellery and other artefacts which enable children to take on the roles of other characters in other situations;
- telephones, books and other resources which actively encourage the children to talk.

Remember that raising the status of talk means finding many ways to communicate to children and visitors that talking is important.

The adult as learner

The adults in the setting should be listening to children and encouraging them towards greater linguistic competence. They should be growing in their ability to articulate the role of talk in children's development and developing processes and procedures for assessing children's needs and planning their future experiences based upon them.

1.8 Planning, assessing and recording

Planning

Planning in the early years, as in any other situation which requires forethought and preparation, depends on those responsible having a clear set of intentions. In the early years setting these will be in response to the needs of the child, and related to the educational aims and objectives of society. The learning outcomes described in the Desirable Outcomes provide the obvious framework for the first steps in planning. But they are only first steps, and will need to be interpreted by the practitioners in relation to their individual settings. Let's explore this suggestion a little.

Suppose we took the phrase 'listen attentively' as an objective relating to story time. It would be simple to attach this to a written plan setting out the processes and procedures of story time and label it as an objective. We have seen many examples of planning which do just this. But we think this is not enough. A plan should enable teaching and learning and at the heart of effective teaching is a clear concept of what is to be learned. The early years practitioners will need to think and talk about the Desirable Outcomes and translate them into a 'do-able' curriculum. This means reaching an awareness of what they mean, how they might be achieved, and what they look like when reached.

For example, does 'listen attentively' mean sitting quietly, or does it involve demonstrating understanding, or both? Does the child listen attentively every time or only when the story is about monsters? How does a child learn to listen attentively? Do we as adults always listen attentively or are we selective?

So, you see, we cannot simply lift the Desirable Outcomes from the page and use them without working on our own greater understanding of them. To further complicate matters, these concepts need to be revisited regularly because they grow with increased knowledge and awareness.

Our first recommendation

Use the Desirable Outcomes for planning, but not without careful consideration of what they mean to you and for your children.

Perhaps, in your consideration, you said that one way children might indicate that they have listened attentively to a story would be if they could recall it. Your learning intention for this activity (and many more like it) might then become 'I/we want the children to be able to reproduce the story of The Three Bears, using puppets, drawings, toys, tape recorder or three chairs'. You will need to consider also at this point what previous experiences the children have had regarding story and puppets, etc., and what support the children will need to enable them to complete the activity: perhaps a period of play with puppets would be of benefit? The bulk of your plans then pay attention to how this might be achieved.

Strategies

By this we mean the decisions that need to be made in order that the activity meets the intention. There are several things which need addressing:

- Which children are going to do this? The whole group or only a small group? (Groupings)
- How long might it take? One session or a series of sessions? (Time)
- How is the task going to be introduced? By the telling of the story? After repeated readings from a Big Book? (Starting point)
- What resources will be needed? Can parents help here? How long will it take to get resources together? (Resources)
- Is the story going to be linked to other learning or experiences? Perhaps a larger topic or series of play activities? (Framework)

Our second recommendation

Give careful thought to how the activity might proceed. Use the above categories (Groupings, Time, Starting Point, Resources, Framework) as a guide to your preparation.

Knowing what you want to achieve (intentions) and how you intend to go about it (strategies) will support the effectiveness of the activity, and if you record this thinking you will have the vehicle for communicating your practice to interested parties, parents for example. Preschool settings are inspected for their implementation of the Desirable Outcomes and OFSTED include nurseries and reception classes in their regular inspection of primary schools. Those who carry out these inspections will require this form of articulation of the activity but the prime purpose of any paperwork must be its usefulness to the adults working with the children, ultimately leading to improved practice.

Our third recommendation

Seek out examples of planning formats already in use and use these by modifying them to suit your own purposes and situations. Evaluate them in terms of how well they support and enhance the activity of the setting, and look for clarity, ease of access, and potential for change and modification. Should you wish to devise your own planning sheets then consider using the headings previously mentioned, namely:

- intentions: i.e. previous experience; what the children will come to know, understand, be able to do; what attitudes are to be fostered; what provision needs to be made to ensure equality of opportunity;
- strategies: i.e. Groupings; Time; Starting Point; Framework; Resources.

As we said before, the plans made are to enable teaching and learning and practitioners will need to monitor and evaluate the activity of the establishment and the achievements of the individual children. It is worth mentioning here that the School Curriculum and Assessment Authority (SCAA) (1996) states clearly that inspection will focus on 'the extent to which the quality of provision is appropriate to the desirable outcomes in each area of learning, rather than on the achievement of the outcomes themselves by children' (p. 3).

The environment seems to be the important element here so you should consider including reference in your planning to the Desirable Outcomes it links to, for example we could adapt our intention to say, 'I/we want the children to be able to reproduce the story of The Three Bears, using puppets, drawings, toys, tape recorder or three chairs' ('children listen attentively ... and respond to story', Desirable Outcomes: Language and Literacy, p. 3).

This particular intention has signalled the possible outcomes of the activity. We are to expect a performance at some time. Working with very young children soon teaches you that very often you get more than you expect. It is wise to try to anticipate unexpected outcomes, since we want to be in a position to encourage and support creativity and experiment. A planning sheet which prompts this thought, perhaps by including the title 'Possible Outcomes', will have added value.

Our final recommendation regarding planning is to remember the five dimensions of learning referred to in section 1. We saw that children's linguistic performance was as much about the surrounding context as their ability. Who they are talking to, why they are talking, and what they are talking about are all powerful influences on how they talk, the vocabulary they use and the fluency of their utterances. The opportunities provided for talk need to be wide and varied; children need 'the challenge of new ideas and concepts, as well as social settings that give support for working on them. Any development and progress in talking will need to be matched against the opportunities provided' (Barrs *et al.* 1990, p. 21).

We can help you monitor your plans and provision by providing you with a checklist of the kind of opportunities you can provide for your children within the curriculum title of language and literacy (Fig. 1.4).

Use this to keep an 'inventory' of the kinds of language and literacy experiences you have and intend to offer your children.

Assessing

When you have given careful consideration to the experiences you offer children, when you have a clear concept of what they might learn and how the activity might progress, then you need to consider how you are going to monitor and evaluate the effectiveness of your provision.

Learning contexts for English	Respond to *i.e. draw, model, role play*	Listen to	Talk about	Write	Play with
1. Stories					
2. Rhymes					
3. Poems					
4. Songs					
5. Pictures					
6. Picture books					
7. Nursery rhymes					
8. Folk tales					
9. Tape recordings					
10. TV programmes					
11. Radio					
12. Telephone					
13. Storytelling					
14. Information books					
15. Word books					
16. Computer data					
17. Diaries					
18. Letters					
19. Accounts of experiences					
20. Recipes					
21. Instructions					
22. Newspapers					
23. Magazines					
24. Books					
25. Games					
26. Guides					
27. Comics					
28. Lists					
29. Captions					
30. Labels					
31. Invitations					
32. Greetings cards					
33. Notices					
34. Posters					
35. Plans					
36. Maps					
37. Diagrams					
38. Catalogues					
39. Jingles					
40. Word games					
41. Riddles					
42. Menus					
43. Signs					

Figure 1.4 Inventory. Use this as a checklist to review the Language and Literacy Curriculum you provide. Aim to provide a variety of contexts for playing with and talking about a wide range of texts.

Ask yourself questions such as:

- What were the children actually doing?
- What were they learning?
- How worthwhile was it?
- What did you (the adult) do?
- What did you learn?
- What contexts, activities or experiences will you plan for next? (Open University 1981, p. 234).

They appear simple at first glance, but they are capable of revealing both the strengths and weaknesses of your practice, and of providing you with a good starting point for future development and modification of the curriculum on offer to children. We suggest you use these regularly. In this way you will get valuable feedback from your observations and reflections.

Evaluation, or assessment, of an individual child's achievements requires observational skills. We will now spend a little time considering observation since it will be the principal vehicle for gathering information on which to base your assessments.

Observation

A key word in association with observation is 'focus'. Most of the pre-thinking described in relation to planning applies here. To begin with you need to have an intention, that is, you need to know why you are observing. There are infinite possibilities – it might be to see whether a child talks to other children, plays with books, chooses pencil play, knows any rhymes, etc. Because there are so many things you can observe, one way of making it manageable is to operate within the principle that you assess what it is you intend the children to learn. So your assessment focus and strategy is decided at the time of planning and is not seen as an additional extra.

Intention
To assess the children's ability to 'recall the story of The Three Bears'. The focus this time is on the recall and not the quality of the puppetry or the drawing.

Strategies
Groupings
Do not try to observe more children than you can manage, bearing in mind what and who you are observing. Sometimes it will be appropriate to observe only one child, at others you may need a larger group.

Time
How much time is available to you? It is sometimes difficult to justify standing back and observing, but it is crucial to do so, and part of your overall responsibility. Remember that you may not need to observe all of an activity. It may be enough to come in at a late stage, or set up a performance stage. Also there may be other adults who can help you.

Starting point
The starting point is in the identification of the intention and in the translation of this to a set of observable features or actions which, in your view, indicate success. It helps

here to prepare a prompt sheet so that you can pick up on the appropriate signals. Perhaps you decide an indication of good recall is to include certain key aspects of the story in a certain order. You could jot these down and use them as an observation checklist.

Resources
You might have a prepared prompt sheet or checklist – be careful to make sure it is related to your planned learning intentions. You might consider taping the talk for support or consideration at a later stage. This can be extremely revealing, but also time-consuming. You will almost certainly need paper and pen.

Framework
The likelihood is that you are gathering information on which to base a judgement regarding the success of your teaching and the child's learning. Your observation notes are better if they record what is seen or heard rather than an interpretation. For example, it is better to note, 'he said, "they all lived happily ever after"' than 'he knows the ending'. The first statement is the evidence or information and the second is the judgement or assessment. Evidence allows for discussion, and this is very important if you are to communicate your assessments to others, or if you wish to compare your assessments with others. Any 'evidence' has the potential to contribute to a profile of the child's development in language and literacy.

Possible outcomes
You should always be alert to the possibility that the child will reveal something unanticipated. If you consider it to be significant, jot down the behaviour so that you can return to it later and consider the implications. Focusing is not about closing options but about being able to sort the significant from the every day indicators of learning.

Language and literacy profile

What we mean by this is a selection of 'evidences' which can be referred to when making an overall assessment of the child's learning. Clearly, if we wanted to assert that a child was able to 'listen attentively' then we would need evidence from more than one occasion. It is not necessary to search for or retain masses of evidence for each child, just enough to enable you, confidently, to make a claim about his/her ability and to back it up with example. Very often you will find the evidence in your memory, but evidence is usually more powerful if it is made concrete in the form of jottings, photographs, tapes and/or samples of the child's work. A useful term to remember when compiling a profile, or record of achievement, is 'snapshot', i.e. a snapshot of the child's development designed to celebrate individual achievement.

Recording

The profile itself is a record, of course. But it is a record of evidence awaiting interpretation. There may be times when you are called upon to record your interpretation or assessment, in other words to indicate what this means in terms of development. Reporting to parents is one possible context for communicating achievement in general terms. Even here there is, at the moment, no requirement to do so in many early years settings. Another possibility is where there may be some cause for concern and the early years practitioner is called upon to make an assessment of the child's development, perhaps for other childhood agencies. In any event there may be times when you need to make a statement about the child's performance and to assist you in this we are including the following *aide-mémoire*.

When recording or reporting a child's attainment in Speaking and Listening comment on some of the following by saying to what extent you believe the child is able to:

- talk spontaneously without asking or prompting
- talk fluently about what s/he is doing
- listen with interest and understanding to adults and other children
- respond to questions
- show in his/her responses an understanding of concepts and information s/he has heard
- take on and use language s/he learns from other children and from adults
- has a sense of audience, expressing him/her self appropriately according to who is listening
- speak clearly and audibly.

In addition, for the multilingual child, say to what extent you believe the child is able to:

- use his/her preferred language(s) freely while working or playing
- switch between languages according to his/her audience
- search for equivalent English words for things s/he can obviously express in a first language
- be prepared to act as support for, or collaborator with, others; enjoy cross-lingual comparisons (Richmond and Savva 1990).

This provides you with a more comprehensive description of linguistic competence than the Desirable Outcomes and, with a selection of evidence, should present an assessment which would more than adequately meet the demands laid out in the Desirable Outcomes should it be considered necessary to apply them to individual children.

2: Story

2.1 Defining terms

This chapter is about the role of story in children's learning and in the early years setting. We have taken, as our guiding framework, the Desirable Outcomes which state that children 'listen and respond to stories' and 'make up their own stories' (p. 3).

Story can make a powerful contribution to the personal, linguistic and conceptual development of the young child. Children should hear stories read aloud and told, and should be encouraged to tell their own stories. In section 2.2 you will find transcripts of children re-telling familiar stories, a valuable precursor to making up their own stories. The language of story helps children to separate language out for closer attention and consideration, thereby enhancing their knowledge and understanding of and about language.

2.2 What children do

We love a good story. We love listening to stories and we love telling them. We love the children's expressions as the giant marches over hill and dale, and as the Prince and Princess kiss. We love getting our tongues round the luscious language of story and we love it when the children join in, clapping, stomping, chanting and whispering their way through the timeless favourites. We love it, mostly the children love it, and we think this is a very good reason to put story high on the early years agenda. But there are other reasons that we could offer in response to the question 'why story?' Storytelling also affects personal, linguistic and conceptual development.

Personal development

Stories enable children to develop their own feelings and emotions by identifying with story characters and plots by proxy. Two children sharing the picture book *Knock Knock Who's There?* talk about how they get scared when they see shadows in the dark. They share what it feels like to be a child imagining witches and monsters in cupboards, under beds, behind doors. They learn they are not alone in these feelings.

Children can reflect on their own and other people's actions, ideas, values, etc., without the risk of actual involvement. After listening to a telling of Jack and the Beanstalk children and adult talk about why Jack's mother was so cross when he traded the cow for five beans. They learn to see other points of view.

Stories enable children to make sense of their own experiences as they report experiences and organise their thoughts in order to communicate them coherently to other people. Imagine that a child is telling an adult about the time when she was a bridesmaid. It was important to her and she includes all the detail about the dress, the bride, the church and her shiny shoes. But she gets muddled about the order of events. She sorts it out by relating it to the purpose of the day – two people getting married – this happened before the ceremony and this happened after. She learns more about the experience by reliving it in her account.

Linguistic development

Stories introduce children to the power of language, as they experience how the creative use of imagery and language can convey meaning and interest to the listener. A small group of children enjoy the story of the Enormous Turnip. They like to join in the bit that goes, 'they pulled, and they pulled, and they pulled ... but still the enormous turnip did not come out'. These words convey the exertion and strength needed to shift what must truly be the largest turnip you ever saw! And how interesting and encouraging it must be to a child to find that here, in this story, it is the smallest character, a mouse, who succeeds where all others, grown-ups included, have failed.

Stories introduce children to new vocabulary and new ways of using language. 'Who's that trip-trapping over my bridge?' 'They rolled their terrible eyes and roared their terrible roars' (Sendak 1963). 'A gentle breeze drifted through the crack. Lucy wedged Pamela's soft body through the opening and then gave her a whack. Pamela went flying out into the quiet night' (McDonald and Pritchatt). Children accommodate new language to their existing repertoire by engaging with it in story.

Storytelling gives children the opportunity to hear the rhythms and patterns of language. Children in the play house are chanting 'by the hair on my chinny chin chin, I shall not let you in'. They are playing with rhythm and rhyme and developing an ear for language. This is the same kind of ear that enables us to recognise spoken French or German even though we may not know the actual words. Children learn to attend to the underlying features of language as well as the words. For it is not just the words that count, is it? Take this phrase as an example, 'do sit down'. Now say it three times giving emphasis to a different word each time. Patterning it differently makes a difference to the meaning. It could be either an invitation or an instruction. Children also learn how different stories 'go', and this will help them gain access to all kinds of books when they are learning to read.

Conceptual development

Stories can introduce children to new ideas and knowledge, helping children to understand new concepts. In a theme 'Pets' children have been read *Dear Zoo* (Campbell) and have made an alternative version entitled 'Dear Pet Rescue' and beginning 'I wrote to Pet Rescue to find me a pet'. In their search for a suitable pet for the nursery they talked about the needs of animals, and whether they should be kept in cages. The story and adult took the children deeper into the subject matter giving them opportunities to explore, reason, and generally think things through.

Stories can introduce children to the cultural traditions and values of the society in which they live: 'and they all went home to tea'; 'and the Prince and Princess were married and lived happily ever after'; 'and the wicked witch was never seen again'; 'and there he found his pot of gold'; 'there were three bears/pigs/sisters/wishes'. We leave you to consider what messages such stories convey about the world in which we live. Through story children can confront and create their world.

Stories can give children the vehicle through which they can explore, hypothesise, plan and predict possible worlds. In Raymond Briggs' *The Snowman* children fly away to a land inhabited by snowmen. Perhaps this kind of imagination contributed to the now almost commonplace explorations of space.

Here is a transcript of a 5-year-old boy, whom we shall call Robert, re-telling the very familiar Goldilocks tale. He has heard it many times, and it is one of his favourites.

Once upon a time there was Three Bears. There was Daddy Bear, there was Mummy Bear, and there was Baby Bear. They had porridge for breakfast every day. One day Daddy said 'Let's go for a walk while our porridge cools'. And there was this girl called Goldilocks. Goldilocks was walking in the forest on her own, she saw the little house, she opened the door, she went in, she saw the porridge. She tasted Daddy Bear's porridge, then next Goldilocks tasted Mummy Bear's porridge, then she tasted Baby Bear's porridge – it was just right. Then she was tired. She tried Daddy Bear's chair to sit on – it was too high! Mummy Bear's chair was too soft! Baby Bear's chair was just right. Then she heard a crash! The chair broke. Then she went upstairs. She tried Daddy's bed, then she tried Mother's bed, then she tried Baby's bed which was just right. She fell fast asleep when she didn't hear the bears come in. They said 'Who's been eating my porridge?' Baby Bear said, 'Who's been eating my porridge and eaten it all up?' And then they went over to the chairs and they said, Daddy Bear said 'Who's been sitting in my chair?', then Goldilocks, then Mummy Bear said, 'Who's been sitting in my chair?' then Baby Bear said 'Who's been sleeping in my bed and who's still sleeping in it?' And when Goldilocks woke up and saw the Three Bears she ran out of the door.

Robert's response to the story was to re-tell it by making a tape for other children to listen to, and his 'telling' was so smooth and confident that we also turned it into a book. Re-telling a story and writing a story are just two ways of securing a response to stories, and indeed other texts. Figure 2.1 sets out the various ways a child in the early years setting might be encouraged to respond. Use this to check that your setting is providing a variety of ways of responding.

Clearly Robert did not make up the above story and some will say that he was simply memorising and repeating the script of a well-known story. If this were the case we should admire his ability to remember. But it is more than an act of reproduction, isn't it? Look at the phrase 'There was this girl called Goldilocks' and 'she fell fast asleep when she didn't hear the bears come in'. You can hear Robert's voice. He is using his own linguistic repertoire to re-tell the story and with encouragement to continue doing so, perhaps changing and developing the story using his voice and his interpretation, he will be doing what all good storytellers do.

Robert worked independently. Children should also be given the opportunity to tell stories in pairs or small groups. Here is the end of another re-telling of Goldilocks told by Edward and Julie:

E: Then they all went upstairs
J: Then
E: No!
J: They didn't ... they forgot ... you forgot ... about the chairs before they went upstairs
E: Whoops a daisy ...
Me: Whoops a daisy, go on then off you go.
E: They ... Father bear tried ... no ... Father bear
J: Goldilocks tried it
E & J: Who's been sitting on my chair? Mother said, 'Who's been sitting on my chair?' Baby bear said 'Who's been sitting on my chair and broke it all up!'

J: Then they come upstairs they do.

E: and then all went upstairs

E & J: 'Who's been sitting on my bed, laying in my bed. Who's been sitting lying on my bed, who's been sleeping in my bed and here she is!' Goldilocks woke up and run downstairs and out of the door.

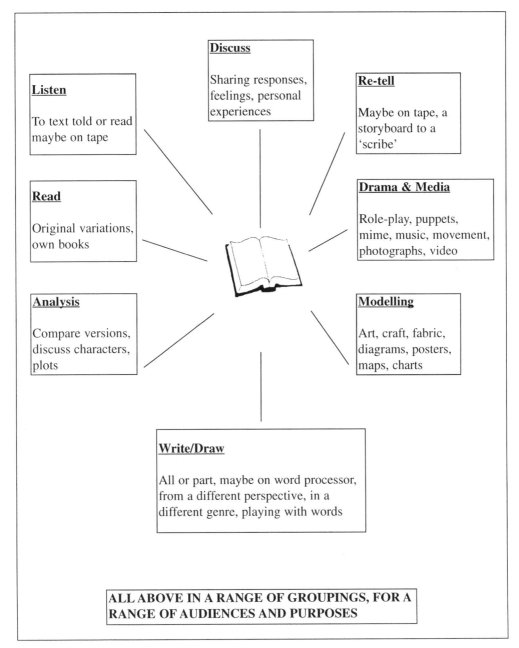

Figure 2.1 Responding to literature

They reach into their knowledge of the story to find the appropriate words. Is it 'sitting on', 'laying in', or 'sleeping in'? Can you see how this kind of activity is calling upon the children to attend to language? Can you also see how Edward and Julie support one another as they work collaboratively to re-tell the story? Collaborative story telling helps children to learn 'to work as part of a group' (Desirable Outcomes, p. 9).

Plan to give your children opportunities to re-tell stories in both independent and group situations, because

> storytelling calls for an active, exacting attention to the world, the very kind of attention which should be at the heart of learning. An invitation to narrate should be seen in the classroom as a call for this high-order attention. Narrative ... digs deep into the linguistic resources of the narrator' (Rosen in Lightfoot and Martin 1988, p. 201).

We said previously that in the re-telling of a story children will be drawing on their linguistic repertoire; they will also be adding to it. You can hear how Edward's experience of stories such as Goldilocks is beginning to influence his own made-up stories in another story he dictated:

The Three Tigers
I am a tiger, Big Daddy Tiger.
I am Mummy Tiger, Little Mummy Tiger.
I am Baby Tiger, Little Teeny Baby Tiger.
I am Great Big Uncle Tiger, who lives in Africa.
Now we go and eat our porridge, to the eaters and to feed some to the Three Bears.
Now we're fighting...
Now we're walking in the forest...
Now we go to our car to drive...
Then we can all go down the hill and up, and up the lanes.
Baby Bear is nervous ... We're not very good at this!'

On the contrary, Edward, you are very good at taking on story language, and knowing stories (and nursery rhymes – 'down the hill and up') will mean that when you come to read them in books you will find the language familiar and will be able to predict what comes next. This will be a great help to you.

Edward and Robert only needed invitations to make up stories; some children will need more support. A good way to encourage children to make up their own stories is to make up stories with them. This is not as difficult as might be imagined if it is accepted that personal stories count. Children are generally very interested in the lives of the adults who work with them. My nursery children used to think that I lived in the nursery and were intrigued by the fact that I had children of my own, that I watched television, that I liked to swim, etc. I have found that telling children my own stories is an excellent way of inviting them to tell theirs. Many of my stories begin with 'I remember when', and the older I get the more stories like this I have to tell. Children of 3 and 4 years of age also have memories, although I can't resist a smile when their story begins 'When I was young'! Such stories, short or long, are valid in their own right. It is, however, a short step from this personal story to the made-up story where the regular daily occurrences can be explored and even made fantastic by the influence of storytelling on language and structure.

The most successful children's authors use familiar events as a foundation for fantasy. Think of M. Sendak's *Where The Wild Things Are* and Max exploring the land of monsters. Think of P. Hutchins' *Rosie's Walk* where Rosie the hen is followed by a scheming fox, and think of *Not Now, Bernard* by David McKee where Bernard is eaten by a monster. All of these stories are embedded in the context of children's daily lives: Max is sent to bed for being naughty, Rosie is out for a pleasant walk, and Bernard's mum and dad are busy watering flowers and hammering nails. These authors have applied what we call the 'what if' principle; what if Max's bedroom were to turn into a forest? what if Rosie sees the fox? what if Bernard gets eaten by a monster? Try this yourself when you are telling your personal stories, ask the children 'what will happen if...?' and you will see how readily they make up stories. Once more we find oracy (story listening) and literacy (story reading) closely interlinked.

We have seen how stories have the potential for personal, linguistic and conceptual development. We have introduced some ways of securing a response to stories and urged you, through example, to encourage children to re-tell familiar stories and to make up stories of their own. Later we will give you some tips for your own storytelling and by the end of this chapter we hope you agree that stories are an excellent resource and that you will be motivated to amass your own repertoire of known stories and build a community of storytellers in your setting.

If, however, you need further convincing of the power of story, try reading the full story of *Cushla and her Books*. It comes from Dorothy Butler (1979) who tells the story of her grandchild. Meek summarises it as follows,

> Her granddaughter, Cushla, declared to be handicapped and retarded by the specialists who saw her after her birth, was solaced from the age of six weeks by her parents reading to her. Later it became clear that Cushla found the stories a world to grow up in when the ordinary world was beyond her physical grasp (Meek 1987, p. 38).

2.3 What the research says

As we discussed in Chapter 1, the Desirable Outcomes for oracy suggest that evidence of progress is a 'growing vocabulary' and 'increasing fluency'. When children hear stories they are certainly introduced to new words and ways of using language which they will not have encountered before. Dombey (in Lightfoot and Martin 1988) tells the story of Anna and her mother sharing *Rosie's Walk* by Pat Hutchins.

> Even in this brief simple text there are words, phrase structures and clause patterns that young children are unlikely to hear in conversation... Nor is she (Anna) discouraged by the density of the clause structure: seven adverbial phrases in the first clause pose no particular problem. Anna is certainly learning new linguistic forms but this is largely a tacit process' (p. 72).

Meek (1988) describes how Ben learned 'how the book works, how the story goes', from reading *Rosie's Walk* and stresses how the lessons he gains from texts will support his development as a reader and writer. But there is even more to it than increasing vocabulary, fluency and book knowledge, important as these are. Stories encourage abstract thought. Wells (1987) offers his account of a 15-year study into the way young children learn to talk and talk to learn. He found a strong correlation between overall success in school and the child's experience of hearing stories read aloud, saying, 'What is so important about listening to stories, then, is that, through this experience, the child is beginning to discover the symbolic potential of language' (p. 156).

Later, when the child enters formal education s/he will encounter many situations where abstract thought will be necessary for learning, where imagination will need to stand in for direct experience. Children with knowledge of story already know that words can 'stand in for' experience, and they can already use words to extend their experiences to accommodate new concepts. This is why many teachers use story as a way in to new ideas and topics for study. *The Lighthouse Keeper's Lunch* has been widely used in primary schools to introduce the scientific study of pulleys, for example.

Listen to some preschool children telling their story to explain why their beans did not grow:

Andy:	Where are the beans?
Wally:	They're invisible.
Andy:	Impossible. They came from a store. Someone took them out.
Teacher:	Who?
Andy:	A robber.
Eddie:	When it was dark a criminal took them.
Teacher:	Why would he do it?
Jill:	Maybe someone came in and said, 'Oh, there's nothing growing. We must take some of them out.'
Eddie:	I think a robber broke in and said, 'They don't need to plant those beans.'
Teacher:	Why would a robber want them?
Wally:	To sell them.
Andy:	Or cook them.
Ellen:	No, maybe to fool people with. See, he could plant them in his garden and when flowers came up people would think he was nice.
Teacher:	If I were a robber I'd take the record player.
Eddie:	Not if you wanted to plant seeds. (Paley 1981, p.58).

Can you see how Paley encourages the children in their story rather than dismissing the idea of a robber as unlikely? Children are very good at telling stories, they just need to know that it is acceptable and that someone is not going to tell them that what happens in their story is silly or unlikely to happen. Remember that they are playing with ideas and testing out possibilities, using language in order to think and learn.

You can write a book, however, about thinking – by recording the conversations, stories, and playacting that take place as events and problems are encountered. A wide variety of thinking emerges as morality, science, and society share the stage with fantasy. If magical thinking seems most conspicuous, it is because it is the common footpath from which new trails are explored. (Paley 1981, p. 4).

The children were further encouraged to explore new trails by working on their stories so that they could be acted out, mostly on the same day and mostly informally. Young children love to act out stories, indeed much of their play is given over to acting out the stories which they experience in everyday life. They act out making dinner and going to work. They act out stories of superheroes. They act out in order to learn and the teacher above recognised this and used what children do naturally to educational advantage. She describes her role as one of helping the children to maintain story structure, and to solve problems. We recommend you read this book which portrays an early years setting where story has become the mainstay of learning across the curriculum and role play has become a principal technique.

We want to spend a little time here talking about 'focusing on language'. In recent years the phrase 'knowledge about language' has entered the vocabulary of teaching and learning. Knowing about language requires that we turn it around on its use and examine it. Let's consider this more carefully. We all use language every day of our lives, and because we are 'expert' users we have an implicit knowledge of it. Most of the time we don't even think about what we are saying or how we are saying it, but sometimes an event makes us stop and consider language itself. Perhaps someone got cross because of the way we said something and on reflection we know we said it in a way that caused misunderstanding. Temporarily we are focusing on language, turning around on it and examining it and its effect; we are making our implicit knowledge explicit.

A vast amount of the knowledge we have about language is not made explicit either to ourselves or to others. Much of it should and will remain inexplicit; there seems to be some that can usefully be brought out in such a way as to add to the interest in language and even to the control of one's own language' (Mittens 1987, p. 10).

I know how I became interested in language. I come from a home where language was fun, we shared jokes, we played language games, we generally used words like toys – to play with. I am in no doubt that this early experience of looking at and considering language in a playful context is directly linked to my chosen profession as a teacher, my move to lecturing in Primary English, and now being co-author of this book. Incidentally, my family still play with language: crosswords, Scrabble, wordsearches, jokes, etc. But there were also occasions in my childhood when language became a topic for analysis, for study. And the main way to study language with very young children is to talk about it.

Stories can be excellent vehicles for talking about language, for helping children find language interesting. When you are sharing stories with children, seek out stories which will invite you and the children to talk about language.

Talk about:

- the different ways people have of speaking. Compare different versions of the same story. Invite people into the setting to tell stories using their individual accent (pronunciation) and dialect (words and word order). Value children's home languages by using them as a positive vehicle for enhancing all children's knowledge about language;
- the way language changes, over time, and according to audience and purpose. Audience and purpose are a concept that is basic to effective communication in

either talk or print. We change the way we talk depending on who we are talking with (for example, we talk differently to our parents and to the bank manager) and why we are talking (for example, to persuade, argue, find out). Talk with young children about the characters in stories and ask 'why did s/he say that?' Perhaps make a poster showing speech bubbles entitled, 'The things monsters say' or 'The things mothers say when they are cross';

- the similarities and differences between speech and writing. Tell a story and then read it and ask the children which they prefer and why. Consider the benefits and weaknesses of each, with a view to helping children to see why it might be better to write the story down in some cases, when we want to tell it to a lot of people who are not with us, for example.

This kind of consideration of language is the foundation of what we might recognise as English in the upper school curriculum. There has been much debate about what children should know about language, and largely this has centred around the topic of 'traditional grammar', and the teaching and learning of language 'rules' (for example, never begin a sentence with 'and' or 'but') and terminology (for example, sentence, verb, object). We recommend that you read *English: Not the Naming of Parts* by Bill Mittens for further discussion of this issue. You will find here, and in many other similar publications concerning knowledge about language, that it is difficult to find direct evidence that this kind of knowledge leads to greater competence. 'Children who learn language most swiftly (i.e. in the first years of speech) do not learn by rule. They learn by need, attempt and learning from experience' (Allen 1987, p.11).

To conclude this section we want to make it absolutely clear that the early years practitioner's primary aim will be to provide contexts in which children can develop their ability to use language. The children's and others' use of language can then be reflected upon so that they can move to greater awareness of the nature and functions of language. Language is a key feature of our environment: as Bain says, 'We teach all sorts of different aspects of our environment. We teach about trees, about towns, about birds, about the weather .... By the same token we need to teach children about language' (1991, p. 14).

2.4 Key concepts

I remember once asking a child if she told stories. Her reply was a disgusted denial that she told fibs (untruths): 'honest, Miss'. It is easy to see how children might interpret the telling of stories to mean telling lies when many adults urge their children away from fantasy and towards 'things that really happen'. This overlooks what must be obvious but which Barbara Hardy made explicit, that:

> We dream in narrative, daydream in narrative, remember, anticipate, hope, despair, believe, doubt, plan, revise, criticise, construct, gossip, learn, hate, and love by narrative. In order really to live, we make up stories about ourselves and others, about the personal as well as the social past and future. (Hardy 1975, p. 13).

In this chapter we see story as including the full range of narrative types from the recounting of experiences that have happened in the child's actual world to the imagined incidences of a possible world. To emphasise our commitment to the variety of stories, long and short, that can be used in the early years setting we offer you the selection of possibilities shown on the scattergram in Figure 2.2.

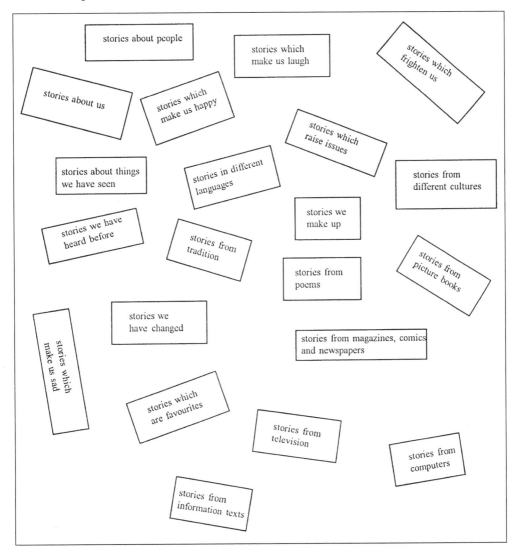

Figure 2.2 Story scattergram

We have talked about the reasons for including story in the early years curriculum and about the potential of story for developing children's interest in language and hence their knowledge of it. Knowledge about language is seen as the opportunities for children to reflect on their own and others' use of language within the framework of a curriculum where early language development is in the provision of experiences where children are called upon to use language to create and communicate meaning.

In line with the Desirable Outcomes, we are not only thinking about the child as the recipient of stories, but as the creator, teller and re-teller of stories.

The following sections offer some practical ways in which story can be used in the early years setting. We urge you to let loose both your own and your children's storytelling.

2.5 Story in play

Much of what might be considered as playing with story will be prompted by the provision made relating to securing children's responses to story. In other words, following a read, told or watched story the adult will encourage children to, in some way, explore the story further in activity. This happens either by direct suggestion, 'I would like you to make a model of Thomas the Tank Engine', or by intervention in the allocation of resources such as a Goldilocks puppet. We have already covered ways in which you might provide for children to respond to texts so there is no need to repeat it here. What we can do is give you the following specific examples of ways in which resources can prompt storytelling. It helps if children have had experience of listening to the types of story you have in mind.

Story box
Purpose
To encourage children to make up their own stories.

Organisation
You will need

- large container (e.g. trunk or plastic dustbin). A black dustbin decorated with gold stars would make an attractive 'Magic Box';
- a variety of artefacts: very large shoe, boot or slipper, bag of coins, large key, feather, jar of pebbles;
- a rug.

Activity
Introduce the box to the children by asking questions: 'What do you think it is? What do you think it is for? What do you think is in it?' Invite one child to pull out one object. Tell your own stories about the object, either personal or imagined. Encourage the children to make up their stories about the single object. Tell the children that you are going to leave the bin and its contents on the story rug so that they can use them to make up their own stories. They will explore the items again, of course, so be close by so that you can pick up in their conversation anything that can be used as a storyline. When the children are ready to present their stories provide them with an audience, either the whole group or a few friends. We are not talking about the kind of audience you would find at the theatre, just a group of people who will listen and respond to the story.

Imaginary journeys
Purpose
To give the children an opportunity to take part in role play.

Organisation
You will need building blocks, a steering wheel, lunch box, tickets, passports and map.

Activity

Using the tickets, passport and map ask the children, 'What is this? What is it for? Who might use it? Why might they use it?' In focused group activity encourage the children to further explore these by making their own. Talk, for example, about why there is a picture in the passport. As the children work together look for a scenario for developing into role play. Someone will undoubtedly mention holidays and trips and this is a good time to 'reveal' the steering wheel and lunch box and suggest that the children use the blocks to make a vehicle which will take them on an imaginary journey.

The story chair

Purpose

To develop children's confidence as storytellers.

Organisation

You will need a small chair, cushion or stool and a soft toy.

Activity

It helps if the soft toy is one which has assumed a definite character in the eyes of the children. You should model telling this toy a story, have it join you at story time, establish the idea that it likes/needs stories. Place the toy on the seat and tell the children that if they want to tell it a story then they can sit on the seat and hold the toy on their lap and whisper a story to it. This makes the situation private and unthreatening . The story can remain a secret between the child and the toy. Gradually suggest that others might like to hear the story, perhaps a close friend or two. As the child's confidence grows s/he might like to re-tell a known story to a larger group. Telling a known story can be less awesome and sometimes children can do this in pairs so that they feel more secure. Confidence here is about finding a non-threatening context in which children can feel what it is like to tell a story to another. This activity can be enriched by occasionally taping the children's stories. This opens up the opportunity for the child to hear the telling and for language to become a focus for discussion. In our experience, when children are confident and happy in the setting storytelling is easy to engineer. Very often the greater difficulty is in getting the children to end their stories!

2.6 Story in focused activities

When children and an adult work together on story a key role for the adult is to help the children get further into the story than they might when working with peers. Any of the activities suggested through our responses to literature diagram will provide this opportunity. Central to this study of literature is the concept that the adult knows the text well and has given some thought to ways in which s/he might support the children in a more analytical and critical consideration of the story.

Figure 2.3 is a picture from a book of rhymes illustrated by Sendak (Sendak 1965) accompanied by the text 'Hector Protector dressed all in green'. You will have read the complete book to the children, perhaps more than once, and you will have encouraged them to explore the picture with questions such as 'what is happening?' and 'why?' They may have written their own versions or made a green collage. The difference between this kind of activity and the one we are describing here is that we are looking for ways of encouraging children to find evidence for their interpretations from the text (which includes the pictures). The key questions in this focused activity are 'how do you know that?' 'how do you know that Hector doesn't like green?' 'what is it about his face that tells you that?' Some response activities might draw children away from the story but what we are talking about here is designed to take them *into* the story. When you are going to join children in their response activity, or when you have arranged for a parent to join them, plan the activity so that its completion depends to some extent on revisiting and challenging the text.

Figure 2.3 Hector Protector illustration

Jack and the beanstalk

Purpose
We want the children to make a critical response to the story.

Organisation
You will need five beans, an imaginative play area decorated with leaves and twigs, dressing-up clothes, pictorial text of Jack and the beanstalk.

Activity
Hide the beans in a container and play a guessing game to gain children's attention.

Reveal the beans saying, 'This reminds me of a story', and ask the children if they know which one. What can they remember about the story? Read from the chosen text in the usual way. Choose/invite a small group of children to join you in the imaginative area to act out this story. Use the text to support the enactment.

Reflection

Following the activity take time to reflect and consider how well the children were able to portray the characters. How did they make the giant scary, the mother cross? Then return to the text and ask similar questions, 'How did the author make the giant seem scary?'

You will see from the above that there is an element of comparison in this activity. Children are comparing their re-enactment with a written text. Comparison is another way of getting further into texts.

Spoken and written versions

Purpose

We want the children to consider the differences between speech and writing.

Organisation

You will need the text from the previous activity plus the confidence to tell the story from memory.

Activity

Read half the story from the text and then tell the rest from memory.

Reflection

Discuss the differences, which the children preferred and why. What can the written version do that the spoken version cannot? How did the author make the giant scary compared with the teller?

Try building up a set of texts that you are comfortable reading and telling so that you can repeat this activity regularly. You should also be aware that increasingly authors are writing alternative versions of traditional tales and here you can compare two texts which may well have quite different emphases. This is not new; the oral story was ever subject to constant change. Consider these three extracts from versions of a familiar fairy tale.

Version 1

There was a woman who made some bread. She said to her daughter, 'Go carry this hot loaf and a bottle of milk to your granny'. So the little girl departed. At the crossways she met Bozo, the werewolf, who said to her, 'Where are you going?'

Version 2

Once upon a time there was a sweet little maiden. Whoever laid eyes upon her could not help but love her. But it was her grandmother who loved her the most. She could never give the child enough. One time she made a present, a small red velvet cap and, since it was so becoming, she always wanted to wear only this.

Version 3

One afternoon a big wolf waited in a dark forest for a little girl to come along and she was carrying a basket of food. 'Are you carrying that basket to your grandmother?' asked the wolf. The little girl said yes, she was. So the wolf asked her where her grandmother lived and the little girl told him and he disappeared into the wood.

Do you recognise this story? How do you know which story it is? What is it in the text that helped you come to this conclusion?

2.7 Story in the environment

This section should really be called storytelling in the environment because we feel that enough has been said in the rest of this book about display and resources. Here, then, are our top ten tips for creating a storytelling setting.

1. Have enthusiasm for telling stories.
2. Have a repertoire of well-known stories.
3. Provide props to support a core of stories. Dressing up clothes which suggest specific stories can be rotated on a regular basis.
4. Provide a range of puppets, both commercially-produced and homemade. Paper bag puppets are probably the simplest to make.
5. Use a tape recorder to enable the recording of stories by adults and children and to provide a useful vehicle for reflection on language.
6. Provide a variety of pictures, postcards, posters and artefacts to stimulate children's telling of personal anecdotes as well as made-up stories.
7. Leave taped stories in a quiet area, sometimes accompanied by the text. This is a useful way of offering children further opportunity of hearing stories read aloud.
8. Have a special place for storytelling: a chair, a rug, a set of cushions set aside specifically.
9. Invite other adults to share their personal stories; sometimes invite a professional storyteller who is used to working with very young children.
10. Provide an appreciative audience. Find ways of encouraging a positive response from other children so that the storyteller wants to go on telling stories.

And here are our top ten tips for storytellers:

1. Start with a well-known story that you yourself enjoy. You could add some nursery rhymes and action rhymes to form a storytelling session.
2. Choose a story with a strong storyline and powerful characters so that you can use your voice and expression to make them come alive.
3. Remember that personal anecdotes are powerful stories and, like a well-known story, can give you confidence because you do not feel you have too much to remember.
4. Prepare your story. Think about how you are going to start and practise aloud, perhaps as you are doing the ironing or cleaning the car. Sometimes it helps to do this in a mirror so that you can see how you will look to your audience. Think also about how you are going to draw the session to a close.
5. To help you to remember the sequence of events in your story try to visualise it. Think of it as a video playing on fast forward where you can see the main events but not the detail.
6. If you need to, note the main events down on small pieces of paper or the back of your hand and use them to sustain your early telling.
7. Think about how you are going to get the attention of your audience. You could use a prop or a visual aid. You may begin by whispering a secret as a way of drawing the children into your story.

8. Use your body. Your eyes are particularly expressive so remember to make eye contact and make your eyes talk. Say the words sad, happy, angry, jolly, foolish, frightening, huge, tiny into a full length mirror. Does your face communicate the meaning of these words and what is the rest of your body doing?
9. Use your voice. Remember that whispers have to be audible. Vary the pitch of your voice from the squeaky mouse to the deep tones of the ugly old troll.
10. Have fun. Enjoy your storytelling, enjoy the responses of your audience as you take them through lands and adventures that no-one else can.

2.8 Planning, assessing, recording and reporting

This section is best read in conjunction with section 8 of chapter 1 which has much to say about planning and assessment in general.

Planning

Planning is about giving curriculum and practice careful thought and adequate preparation. Some plans will be recorded but much of what happens in the early years setting will be spontaneous and stimulated by the children's own interests and needs. This does not mean that such activities do not require careful thought, however, just that it would be impossible to record every aspect of every minute of activity. Many of the daily occurrences will not need detailed plans, but all benefit from forethought. Story and story time should be part of the daily routine of the nursery, yet it is this routine itself which can be a threat to the way in which story works for children. It is easy for it to become a habit where reasons for reading or telling a story are no longer articulated. On the one hand we celebrate the fact that children are being read/told stories frequently and that stories form part of the fabric of the environment. On the other we can see that story can be at risk of becoming stale through lack of monitoring and development. Let's look at some of these potential risks now, but in a positive rather than negative frame, by answering the question, 'How can we keep story alive?'

Articulate the rationale for story in the early years curriculum
It is a matter of professional obligation that we communicate regularly to ourselves, our colleagues and our community that story is important. For all the reasons set out earlier, story is more than an easy option. Of course, there is enjoyment and an almost unique sense of togetherness when a story is shared. But there can and should also be times of endeavour, challenge and uncertainty. The place for this overall statement regarding the value of story in general is in a policy statement. That statement does not have to be a meticulously crafted, lengthy document unless this is what the members of the setting prefer. A policy needs to be an explanation of what goes on in the setting, why it goes on, and where it is heading. It also needs to be easily modified and changed as practice changes. This can be achieved through photographs accompanied by verbal or written commentary. Consider, for example, the message conveyed by the picture in Figure 2.4.
    A living policy indeed!

Monitor story provision
Make sure that the 'diet' of story represents the variety and range previously outlined. How about keeping a tally on the stories children encounter against the list set out earlier in this chapter, say over one term, to see whether you are achieving a balance?

Any omissions will then be in your consciousness and you can take steps to rectify them. Perhaps this list could be included, with your own additions, of course, in your policy? Make sure that the stories you plan to offer are not limited in type and style.

Figure 2.4 Adult and child sharing a book

In tandem with monitoring story provision, monitor also the kinds of responses that the children are encouraged to make. For example, how often do you encourage them to role play in response?

Value story
Your policy statement, resources, time allocation, and activity will all communicate how much you value story. One of the greatest evidences of the role of story in your setting will be carried in the children's voices. They will be your advocates as they tell parents and friends about:

- their favourite stories
- the visitor who came to tell stories
- the imaginary play area set out as a house made of straw
- the giant boots for dressing up
- the time they told their stories to older children
- the time they acted out their story on the magic carpet
- the time they had a story parade and all dressed up as book characters.

All of the above require careful planning and the principles set out in section 1.8 are equally important here:

- Have well thought out aims and objectives, or as we prefer to call them, intentions.
- Think in particular of how these intentions will become practice. Especially give

detailed planning consideration to groupings, time, starting points, resources, framework and possible outcomes.

When you have invested the time to think, resource, prepare and evaluate a story activity don't discard all your efforts. Why not replace any used resources and put your plans, etc. together to build up a set of activities for future use? They may only need slight modification to make them suitable for a different group of children.

Assessing

As stated in Chapter 1, you assess what it was you intended the children to learn. If you intend them to learn that story is enjoyable then you need to think about what the possible indicators of enjoyment could be. Here are some possibilities which come immediately to mind:

* asking for a story to be read or told
* talking about favourite stories
* engaging with a story by smiling, nodding, laughing, sighing, questioning, challenging
* using story in play, by drawing, modelling, acting out
* bringing in stories from home.

When you observe these behaviours then you will have evidence to answer the question: 'to what extent can I say that s/he enjoys story?'

This is a simple example of the process you need to go through in order to prepare yourself for the strategies you might use for assessment. Most of the above will be obtained by observation of the children at play and sampling the products of their learning, but we have left out one strategy which is often neglected. You could ask the child!

A word here about using questioning as a strategy. You could ask the child the simple, closed question, 'Do you enjoy stories?' The answer could be as short as 'Yes' or 'No', and you must ask yourself whether this is enough to enable you to make a judgement. Hopefully, if your setting is geared for talk, the child will volunteer more, and even give you a detailed description of his/her attitude to story. Another child may not be so forthcoming and you could consider enabling questions such as, 'Do you have a favourite story?' and 'What did you think of the ending?' You must decide when you have enough evidence to say something specific about the child's response to story. There is no guarantee that you will get it exactly right, all you can do is give the child and the focus thoughtful consideration, and then make the assessment. Confidence grows with experience.

Recording and reporting

Chapter 1 gave you some prompts which you could use to record children's progress in speaking and listening in general. Some statements will be particularly useful here, for example a sense of audience will be relevant to story telling. You could and should add your own prompts according to your planned intentions and they will very likely be related to the learning potential of story as set out in section 2.2. Your learning intentions relating to language and story might include any of the following. We want the children to learn to:

* take on story language

- give characters different voices
- make stories
- change and re-shape known stories
- use intonation and pitch to add emphasis
- show understanding of a story through a variety of responses
- have a selection of favourite stories
- know a range of story types
- convey meaning through a variety of narrative forms: anecdote; accounts; personal experience, etc.
- use story structure, with a clear beginning, middle and end.

You then use the intention as a focus and gather evidence which enables you to make an assessment answering the question, 'To what extent can I say that ... the child takes on story language?' or 'gives characters different voices?' or 'makes up stories?'

When you want or need to record your observations remember to include the date of the observation/sample. Note the learning context, i.e. what was happening (play with farm animals) and the social context, i.e. who with (in pairs); the purposes. You need to note the context and purpose since, as we saw in Chapter 1, they make a difference to how you interpret the evidence.

One further, but significant, point is that how you interpret the evidence must make a difference to what you do. One of the key principles of assessment is that it informs future teaching and learning. Think of assessment as a way of getting to know your children, what they know, think, and can do. The better you know the children, the better you will be able to provide the appropriate learning experiences.

We leave this chapter with the words of the storyteller B. Rosen who writes,

For everyone is a storyteller and, given some nurturing, can become a better one. ... once set loose, the storytelling impulse enables the most unlikely people to deploy unsuspected linguistic resources and strategies. (1988, p. 167).

3: Books

3.1 Defining terms

In any early years classroom you can see books: books in a reading corner, books as part of a display, books on the teacher's shelf and often books just lying around on tables and even the floor. Books, however, are not the only form of the written word to be seen: words will cover every part of the room, labelling, describing, questioning, reminding, instructing, informing and entertaining. The Desirable Outcomes require children, among other things, to 'enjoy books'. This chapter considers how that can come about in an early years classroom and what we know about young children and books. We use 'books' in a very generous way to include all examples of the written word, i.e. texts that may be found in the classroom.

3.2 What children do

Children are never too young to benefit from books. The young baby often sees a book as a physical object and will put it straight into the mouth or play with it in the bath along with the plastic duck. Even at these early stages children learn how to handle books – that pages can be turned, that you can read on and look back to check and, through using the pictures as a guide, that there is a right way up for books.

At this stage the book is just another physical object or toy but the young child is learning how books are organised. Many books for young children have flaps to lift, squeakers to press and holes through which to poke fingers. As well as being great fun, the children are also learning that looking at a book is an active process; it's not something that you sit back and have done to you but it is something where you get involved.

That involvement can take a great many forms. Often the young child will enjoy labelling the pictures in the book. A two-year-old will eagerly point to a picture of a tree in the book and then immediately point through the window to the tree in the garden. Connections are being made between the representation in the book and the actual object in real life – an important lesson to be learned by the young reader.

Another way in which young children become involved in books is by telling the story themselves. The book may be one which they have heard several times and so know the story well or the pictures may tell a clear story and so become the basis for their reading. In both cases the story which the young child reads may bear little or no resemblance to the story as printed but the child is demonstrating an understanding that books contain something meaningful and enjoyable and that the reader can bring his/her own understanding of life to a book.

For many young children the most enjoyable feature of a book is that it gives you the undivided attention of an adult. The warm lap, the arm held tightly around you or the comfortable bed as sleep gradually takes over, all serve as valuable lessons about the security and warmth of looking at books. Reading is an interpersonal activity and the young child learns within a secure and pleasurable context.

The adults in a young child's life also play an important role as models of reading behaviour. The child who sees adults, whether at home or at school, reading or enjoying books will not only learn book handling skills but will also learn that reading is a valuable activity to which it is worth giving your time.

Figure 3.1 Parent and child reading newspapers

3.3 What the research says

An enormous amount of research has been done into early reading and much of it has been highly influential on practice. Shirley Brice Heath (1983) looked at children learning literacy at home and at school in two different communities in America. 'Roadville' was a traditional well-established white working-class community and 'Trackton' a black working-class community with a history of farming. Both communities were literate but had very different attitudes to reading and writing. Heath comments, 'For Roadville the written word limits alternatives of expression; in Trackton, it opens alternatives. Neither community's ways with the written word prepares it for the school's way' (p. 235).

The work of Heath tells us that children come into the early years classroom having had experiences of books and having learned about the roles of books in their lives but this learning may or may not match the expectations of the setting they enter. It is the responsibility of the adults within that setting to recognise and respond to their understanding and we shall consider how later.

Barrie Wade and Maggie Moore (1996) have done a longitudinal study of the effect that books can have on the learning of very young babies. They found that the long-term effect on children as they entered nursery and then school was extremely significant. Experience of books from a young age enables children to make connections and so to take control of their reading. Carol Fox (1993) saw how Josh in his pre-sleep monologues was making many allusions to books he had read and stories he had heard. 'Intertextuality' is a feature of many powerful texts (when a writer alludes to other texts) and the reader who is familiar with a wide range of books has greater knowledge at his/her disposal to facilitate reading.

Margaret Meek (1988) talked about the 'reading lessons' that texts give. She showed how an effective text can support the inexperienced reader and guide him/her through the book. For example, look how in *Rosie's Walk* Rosie always walks from left to right, encouraging you to turn over and look at the next page. Texts can also support readers through the language they use, the content and concepts they contain and the way in which they are laid out on the page. The National Literacy Project (1997) sees learning to read and talking about reading as happening at three levels: text, sentence and word. In this chapter we are discussing the text level, i.e. the understanding of the whole or the 'big shapes' (Barrs and Thomas 1991).

Ferreiro and Teberosky (1983) studied young children's learning of literacy before they started school and concluded that 'reading is not deciphering' and so is not best learned through deciphering exercises. Henrietta Dombey (1992) identified the lessons that young children need to learn to become effective readers. One of these was 'how to use the larger patterns and structures of the written word to make sense of the text' (p. 14).

The question which must follow is how do children come to learn these things? The research we have already mentioned gives some indication of the lessons that are learned through 'literacy events' in the home. These lessons are powerful and need to be built on in the early years classroom.

Holdaway (1979) outlines the strategy of using big books as a way of bringing into the classroom that intimate sharing of a book that often takes place, for example, at bedtime. Over many years (Southgate and Arnold 1981, OFSTED 1996) research and evidence from inspection have criticised the fact that many teachers rely too heavily on reading with individual children (often known as 'hearing readers') rather than planning for focused group and class activities. Key teaching sessions can make much of the implicit knowledge of young children explicit and so enable it to be extended. Cambourne (1997) identified four dimensions of effective learning activities (Table 3.1).

Cambourne argued that successful learning activities, among other things, were preceded by an explicitly stated purpose for engaging in the activity. This can involve a high degree of modelling and what he describes as 'thinking aloud' by the teacher. We shall be exploring how this works out in practice later in the chapter.

Explicitness	as opposed to	Implicitness
Structure	as opposed to	No structure
Planning		Random
Systematic		Learn-by-chance
Mindfulness	as opposed to	Mindlessness
Contextualised	as opposed to	Decontextualised

Table 3.1

3.4 Key concepts

Handling books

One of the most obvious points which needs to be made about books in the early years classroom is that they must be there. There needs to be a range of genres so that children meet as many different types of book as possible. These may include

- rhyming story books
- alphabet books
- picture books
- wordless picture books
- cumulative stories
- books that deal with important themes
- non-fiction
- books where the illustrations matter
- books which draw on existing knowledge, books with rhythm and rhyme and, last but not least, books made by the children themselves.

And so we could go on. The books in the classroom need to be there and to be available to children so they will learn book handling skills, come to enjoy books and to see them as friends (Bromley 1996).

Responding to books

Research and experience shows us that children come with different understandings and expectations of the role books play in their lives. Some will have seen adults relaxing with a book and heard them discussing the plot or characters of the latest novel they are reading; others will have seen adults cast a cursory glance over the newspaper headlines and nothing more, and for others the written word will be sacred and must be accepted without question. These culturally learned values will impact on children's attitudes and responses to books in the classroom.

Secondly, we must never forget the affective nature of books. In books we can escape the harsh reality of life, explore possibilities, identify and come to terms with strong feelings – the same can happen for children.

Making sense of books

When we read we are attempting to discover the meaning the author had in mind when writing the text and by relating that to our own understandings we attempt to make sense of what the book is about. We draw on our existing knowledge of the world (semantic), of language (syntactic) and of the sound–symbol relationships in print (graphophonic). Learning to read involves using different skills, knowledge and understandings explicit in a variety of ways which we shall now go on to identify.

3.5 Books in play

We have already described an early years setting which is full of all different kinds of books. If this is the case, children will become familiar with books and will naturally begin to include them in their play.

Home corner

Hall (1987) has already described in detail the value of making a home corner into a literate environment and the strong impact on children's play. Some children in a nursery class were observed during the course of a morning in a 'literate home corner'.

Paul sat in the armchair with his legs crossed avidly reading a copy of *The Guardian*. He turned over the pages one at a time scanning each from top to bottom and left to right.

Andy flicked through the pages of the phone directory until he found the page he wanted. He ran his finger down a column of names, stopping at one two thirds of the way down and referring to it as he dialled the number and made his phone call.

Theresa was cooking. She looked carefully at the recipe book and then in the cupboard. She took a piece of paper and pencil and copied something from the recipe book. She then gave this list to Susie, sending her off to shop for the missing ingredients.

Maria lay down on the bed, choosing a magazine from the pile at the side to look at while she was 'feeling poorly'.

These children were using 'books' for all the different reasons adults do and they were doing this within a meaningful context. They were learning what it is like to be a reader.

Imaginative play

It is not only within the context of home play that books can play a central role.

A reception class was doing a topic on water and had turned the imaginative play area into a hairdressers. Within this area they had put several different sorts of texts:

- magazines for the customers to read
- magazines from which the customers chose their new hairstyles
- books which told the hairdressers how to do the hairstyles.

In setting up this context some very lively discussions were held by the children on the sorts of reading materials that would be in a hairdressers. They had brought in a variety of magazines from home but several of these were rejected as not being suitable, according to the criteria established by the children, based on their own experiences of hairdressers.

This is just one example of the sort of imaginative play context where books can play an integral part. Others could be a restaurant or cafe, a travel agent, a newsagent or even a bookshop.

Silent reading

Many schools have a time during the day when everybody in the school reads. This is variously known as:

USSR   Uninterrupted Sustained Silent Reading
ERIC   Everybody Reading In Class
SQUIRT   Sh! Quiet! It's Reading Time.

The rationale behind this is that it gives children time and opportunity to browse and read; it shows that reading is valued and it allows all children to see adults reading for pleasure. Even very young children can value the time and opportunity to concentrate on a book.

Figure 3.2 A very young child reading

Even young children in nursery and reception classes can benefit from a reading time. Don't expect it to be quiet, however, and keep it to a maximum of ten minutes.

It is helpful either to put a selection of books out on each table or to allow each child to choose a selection before reading time starts. They will want to talk and share their books with each other and the adults and you can also take the opportunity to enthuse about books you are reading with them.

Drama/role play

Books can often be used as a starting point for drama and/or role play. You may find that children spontaneously act out well-loved stories and as a teacher you can both support and extend this in several ways.

One nursery teacher, without any initial comment, put out on a table three bowls, three spoons, three chairs and three pillows. Immediately a group of children took these and started playing out the story of Goldilocks. After several minutes of play, a nursery nurse sat down at the table with a book of the story. The children asked her to read the story which she did with many interruptions as the children compared their version with that of the book. At the end of the reading the nursery nurse withdrew and the children resumed their play, adding many more details.

If children are familiar with a book it can be extended in several ways. Ask the children to imagine what happened before the book started (What was Rosie doing before she went on her walk?), after it ended (What did mummy and daddy say to Maisie Middleton when they got up?) or filling in gaps in the story (Why did Hairy Bear's children decide to get food from the fridge?).

The book area

This should be an important feature of any classroom, providing a secluded and comfortable place for children to browse. In an ideal situation it would include bean bags and/or large cushions, display about books and books arranged as far as possible with the covers showing. It may well be that you do not have all your books in the book area at one time; rotating them can maintain interest and motivation.

The arrangement of the book corner can draw children in to books in a variety of ways. Graham and Kelly (1997) describe how after reading many books about bears the children's particular favourite was *Can't You Sleep, Little Bear?* by Martin Waddell and Barbara Firth.

> it was not long before a dark cave appeared in the corner of the classroom with a little bear within. At the entrance to the cave was a notice 'Please take the torch and a bear book and read to Little Bear' (p. 51).

Other teachers have turned book corners into witches' caves (Meg and Mog books), boats (*Mr Gumpy's Outing*) and even large dustbins (*This is the Bear*).

3.6 Books in focused activities

The previous section looked at ways in which books can become a part of both spontaneous and structured play activities. We now go on to look at planned focused teaching activities whose purpose is the teaching of early reading skills and understandings.

Big books

We have already seen how Holdaway's (1979) work has encouraged teachers to use enlarged texts with a group of children in order to focus attention on particular aspects of print. Here we will consider how big books can help children to use their semantic knowledge to predict and make sense of the book as a whole. In following chapters we shall consider using big books to develop word recognition and phonic and graphic knowledge. It is important to remember that one focus is enough for a session and, whatever the teaching point, it must be done within the context of enjoying the book as a whole.

Here is an outline of a focused teaching time using the enlarged text of *Each Peach Pear Plum* by Janet and Allan Ahlberg (1978)

Purpose
To show the children that their existing knowledge can help them make sense of a text.

Organisation
The children are seated so that each child can easily see the enlarged text.

Activities
Read the text on each page quite quickly and then concentrate on looking at the pictures and discussing them. For example, on the first page look at the fruits in the trees to identify them – it would be helpful to have some examples of the real fruit the children could match with the pictures. Can you spy Tom Thumb? Where is he? Why do you think he is called Tom Thumb? Don't spend a lot of time on each page but

Figure 3.3 Shared reading

follow up the children's interests, reminding them of the stories and rhymes which they may already know. What is Bo Peep looking for? Who knows a rhyme about Bo Peep? Let's say it together so we can remember what she has lost. Do you think she is going to find them?

Once you have gone through the book talking about each picture, read it again quite quickly to re-establish the sense of the whole. You will probably find that some children will read along with you. Remind them at the end that they knew a lot of the rhymes and stories that are talked about in this book and that helped them to understand the story.

Group reading

When I was in school I remember group reading as an incredibly boring activity; about five of us sat around a table, each with a copy of the text, taking it in turns to read a page. I always used to get into trouble for reading ahead and losing the place. The group reading we are talking about here is not like that!

Purpose
To help the children to use pictures to predict and infer.

Organisation
A small group of children sat around a table with an adult, each with a copy of the text *Sunshine* by Jan Ormerod (Picture Puffin 1981).

Activities
Tell the children that the book is called *Sunshine* and was written by Jan Ormerod. Ask them to look at the front cover and try to work out what the book is going to be about.

What is the daddy doing? What do you think the little girl is going to do the sunshine in this picture?

Go through each page asking the children to tell you what is happening going to happen and on what basis they are making those decisions.

After the session make sure a copy of the text is in the book corner; you may well find that children will go back to it and often 'read' it to their friends.

Reading enrichment

Frequently texts can be used as a starting point for other activities which can enhance children's appreciation and enjoyment of the book. Reading enrichment activities can take many forms:

- drawing a map or time line of the story
- putting the book into picture strip form
- making a collage of a particular scene
- sequencing pictures from the book
- making a book into a play script
- making mood faces
- making puppets and acting out the story.

At all points during the activity it must be remembered that the purpose of the activity is to increase children's understanding of the text. Therefore discussion is vital so that an adult's comments and questions can focus thinking. For example:

- What happened before that?
- What did she feel like when that happened?
- Where was he standing?
- Who was in the room with him?
- What did she say to him?
- Why do you think they did that?

Reading to the class

You can never read too much to children. It is through listening to books being read to them that children begin to appreciate literary or book language. The first page of *Peace at Last* by Jill Murphy says 'The hour was late'. We would not normally speak in that way and it is through listening to books read aloud that children will begin to get a feel for the pattern and rhythms of book language. Listening to an 'expert' reading aloud also demonstrates to children the use of expression, intonation and pace and gives them a model for their own reading.

Planning for storytime is as important as for any classroom activity. In your planning you will need to take account of the following.

The book you will read

Reading to children is a valuable way of broadening their experience of literature. Your medium and long-term plans need to take account of the range of texts they will encounter and in the short term you can build on current interests and enthusiasms.

The time of day

The end of the day or session is often a good time to gather the class around a book; it affirms the class identity and calms everyone down before going home. However, the

Figure 3.4 Child's drawing of Goldilocks

calming effect can be too powerful! The day is a long and busy one for young children – Lewis's mum regularly had to come in and carry him home as he fell asleep during the story. Consider starting the day with a story when the children are fresh or during the middle of the day as a consolidation of work done.

The resources you will need

Puppets, pictures, artefacts, clothes will all add to the power of the story. Look ahead and consider what will add to your book reading. Remember, however, that you are your biggest resource. Practise reading aloud (shut yourself in the bathroom if necessary!) using expression, volume and pace to make the effect you require.

The introduction and conclusion

It is important to place the book into a context for the children. 'This book is called *Alfie Gets In First*. Can you remember other books we've read about Alfie? This is another book by Pat Hutchins. Do you remember she wrote *The Doorbell Rang*?' You might use the front cover to predict what the book is going to be about.

At the end of the story you might want to:

* review the story (who came to Kipper's birthday party?)
* respond to it (do you think Rosie knew the fox was following her?)
* evaluate it (do you think Maisie Middleton really had all that for breakfast?) and even
* begin to criticise (do you think that would really have happened?).

Discussion issues

Be careful not to interrupt the flow of the story with too many explanations. Frequently the context of the whole story will make difficult words or phrases clear. Don't be tempted to rewrite the text, an author will have spent a long time choosing words carefully; if you are tempted to do this then perhaps the book you have selected is not appropriate at this time.

Other activities

It is often useful to have a selection of poems, rhymes, finger rhymes and/or action songs ready for any spare time. They can also serve usefully to remind children of the theme of the story.

3.7 Books in the environment

We have already discussed the range of books that should be in an early years classroom and the programme of study for Key Stage 1 gives a useful starting point for this. Books, however, are expensive and take up a large part of a budget so it is important to be clear about what we are looking for when selecting. There was a time when the choice was between a 'scheme' or 'real books'. Today that distinction is not a valid one. The days of sterile repetitive texts are, thankfully, passing and many of the more recent schemes (e.g. Cambridge Reading 1996) contain some high quality texts. What do you look for when you are selecting books for the classroom? We shall try to identify some general principles.

Selecting books for the classroom

Emotional truth (Graham and Kelly 1997)

A 'good book' for any age is one which strikes a cord in the heart. *Not Now, Bernard* by David McKee is about feeling insignificant and unnoticed, *Titch* by Pat Hutchins is about being the youngest and always getting left behind and *Can't You Sleep, Little Bear?* by Martin Waddell and Barbara Firth is about the fear of the unknown. Children's and adult literature all deal with these themes because they are universal to the human condition. In a good book one can recognise oneself and come back again and again to find new insights.

Language
Contrary to popular belief, short sentences make a book harder rather than easier to read. A good test is to try and read a book aloud; a book whose language sounds natural and has its own rhythm, pattern and maybe rhyme is one which will support the inexperienced reader.

Illustrations
The illustrations can serve a variety of purposes in a book. In some cases they are just pictorial representations of what is in the text but in others they carry as much meaning as the story, if not more (e.g. *Rosie's Walk, Granpa, You'll Soon Grow Into Them, Titch*). Books like these can be very supportive to inexperienced readers; they enable them to read the story independently and even on occasion to be more 'in the know' than the person reading only the words. As adults we often do not give enough time to the illustrations and would do well to learn from young children's attention to detail.

Significant authors
There are many authors who consistently catch the moment in their writing for young children. As you read and build up your own bibliography you will get to know some of these names. Your list will probably include, among others, Alan and Janet Ahlberg, Pat Hutchins, Shirley Hughes, Tony Ross, John Burningham, Mick Inkpen, Nick Butterworth, Michael Rosen, Sarah Garland, Sara Hayes, Jill Murphy, Martin Waddell.

Don't forget that for the children in your class the most significant authors will be themselves. Include in all your book collections examples of books written by the children themselves, either independently or during a shared writing activity.

Cultural diversity
You will naturally want to ensure that all children in your class receive positive role models from the books they read. Therefore you will choose books that portray a wide variety of lifestyles, that reflect different cultural values and beliefs and also different print systems (e.g. dual language texts).

Environmental print
At the start of this chapter we said that we were using the term 'book' in the most generous sense to include all aspects of written language. We have discussed the value of the literate environment in imaginative play and other aspects of print in the classroom can provide effective learning opportunities.

Labels
Labels which ask questions or make statements can help children develop a sight vocabulary. If you highlight the key word, the context will help understanding and the highlighting will help remembering. Changing the labels will focus attention, e.g. What is in the *cupboard*? is changed the next week to Put the puzzles in the *cupboard*.

Display
Effective display is that which involves the children by requiring them to make a response. A nursery class had made a huge junk robot. One evening the teacher

displayed this against the wall and put a huge speech bubble coming out of his mouth.

The children made several suggestions and then voted. The teacher wrote their suggestions in a letter to the robot during a focused shared writing activity. The next day the robot replied

Other displays will have a specific reading focus:

- an author of the week
- a book of the week
- a letter of the week with a display containing soap, scissors, sandwiches, sticky tape, etc.

Notice boards
Many classrooms will have a notice board which acts as a source of information to the adults who come into the class and for parents. This can serve as a useful demonstration to children of the purposes of print but will have to be made explicit to them, 'I'm putting up this notice to remind everyone we're going on a trip tomorrow'.

Organisation

Books will be displayed attractively and invitingly with frequent changes to maintain interest. If you have a local library this can also be a useful resource. Iris was the local librarian who encouraged the children to look at all the books on the shelves, showed them how they could find out where to put them back and read stories to them. Through Iris the children learned that libraries were not intimidating but vast treasuries of delight.

3.8 Planning, assessing and recording learning

The Desirable Outcomes specify the required learning outcomes for children. In this chapter we have been focusing particularly on the following areas which can be expressed in terms of intentions or aims. We want the children

- to enjoy books;
- to handle books correctly;

- to understand the different purposes for reading;
- to know how books are organised;
- to know that words and pictures carry meaning;
- to know how print is read in English.

Once you have identified your learning intentions you then need to know whether they have been fulfilled and in order to do this we need to decide what will be the evidence of learning. What will tell us that the children have achieved what we wanted them to achieve? There are different ways of gaining evidence of learning and each method will give us different information.

Observation

As part of our daily classroom life teachers need to take time to observe children's behaviours. As they observe they need to ask questions which will direct them to the required learning:

- Do the children choose to look at books?
- Do they handle books carefully and appropriately?
- Do eye movements indicate that they follow the text from top to bottom and left to right?
- Do the children turn to books for information?

Conversation

From time to time you need to hold conversations with individual children about reading and their attitudes to it. Do you enjoy reading? What are your favourite books? Why? Answers to questions such as these will demonstrate how children feel about books and reading.

Booksharing

Monitoring individual and small group booksharing lessons will give you useful information about the skills and understandings the young child is bringing to reading. Is the child able to tell the story from the pictures? Does the child know the difference between the text and the pictures? Can the child draw on existing knowledge to make sense of a book?

Once all this information has been collected an appropriate format for recording it needs to be found. Many schools and settings establish their own format and several have been published. Two of the most useful are *The Primary Learning Record* (CLPE 1993) and those published by the Reading and Language Information Centre (University of Reading 1995). With very young children, whatever format one selects for recording it is essential to have some means of catching those magical moments of insight which are so crucial to those wanting to start where the child is and lead him/her on. Teachers have adopted various strategies for this: carrying around a reporter's notepad and pencil, an index card box with a card for each child, writing a paragraph about each child at the end of every week, focusing on a few children each day.

Planning

It might seem strange to end the chapter with a section on planning as it is such a vital element of effective teaching and learning. Planning for books can be difficult because to a certain degree much of what has been discussed is going on in most early years classrooms all the time. However, planning must be done for focused learning which may come through planning of resources, environment or focused teaching. The National Literacy Project (1997) offers a framework for planning for both medium and short term.

The chapter began by saying that books can be found in most early years classrooms. It is hoped that the rest of the chapter has shown that it is not enough to just have the books there. Careful planning needs to take place to ensure that the books there are the most appropriate and that they are used effectively as part of the process of teaching reading and making readers.

4: Rhyme and Rhythm

4.1 Defining terms

If you go into any playground or park where you hear young children playing you will hear rhyme and rhythm. For such is the stuff of language. Young children almost instinctively make up nonsense verses, playing with the sound and pattern of language. The Desirable Outcomes require children to 'begin to associate sounds with patterns and rhymes' and to 'listen and respond to stories, songs, nursery rhymes and poems'. This chapter begins to explore how this can take place within an early years setting and how it forms the foundation of literacy learning.

4.2 What children do

I found a box of matches
Behind the kitchen door door door,
But when I went to pick them up
They all fell on the floor floor floor.
Singing aye aye yippee yippee aye
Apple pie.
Singing aye aye yippee yippee aye
Apple pie.
Singing aye aye yippee
Going to the chippy
Singing aye aye yippee yippee aye
Apple pie.

I asked my five-year-old daughter to tell me some of the rhymes she and her friends sang in the playground and that is the one she chose to sing to me. She had little sense of what it meant and could only remember it by continually going back to the beginning and singing the whole. It is clear that what is important here is not the meaning but the rhyme, rhythm and repetition of the language.

This fascination is echoed by very young children as they gradually become proficient in making the sounds of language. They play with them, exploring different sounds, initially to find out what they can do with their voices and then to test out the responses of others to the sounds they make. This playing with sounds then evolves into nursery rhymes, action songs and conversational play. The popularity of the Teletubbies is just one example of children's delight in the sound and the rhythm of language, where the meaning becomes subservient to the sound.

4.3 What the research says

Phonology is the study of the sound system of a language. Part of becoming an effective language user is the ability to hear the sounds of the language. Words are the largest units of sound into which we can break language down and surprisingly perhaps they are difficult to distinguish in spoken language. Listen to someone talking in a language which is not your first language and you will experience how difficult it is to identify separate words. It can be difficult even in a different dialect. I once went into a fish and chip shop in the Black Country and completely failed to understand the lady behind the counter – I had to retire defeated and cook myself bacon and eggs! There are no spaces between words in spoken language; we identify them by their meaning and the stress and intonation of the speech.

We can break words down into syllables and these are the rhythm or beat of language. The easiest way of identifying the syllables in a word is by clapping the beat and young children enjoy doing this, feeling the rhythm of the language as they do so.

Syllables can be further broken down into what we call onset and rime. The onset of a syllable is the initial sound before the first vowel (a,e,i,o,u) and the rime is what follows. For example, 'dog' is one word of one syllable; the onset is 'd' and the rime is 'og'; similarly 'ship' is one word of one syllable where the onset is 'sh' and the rime is 'ip'. Research (Chukovsky 1963, Bryant and Bradley 1985) identified how important early experiences of rhyme are for language learning and especially through the knowledge of nursery rhymes. Goswami and Bryant (1990) and Goswami (1994) have shown how children use their knowledge of rhyme in reading development; their understanding of common letter strings which form the patterns of words that rhyme help them to create word families and learn new words by making analogies with known ones.

With very young children the most important aspect is raising their awareness of the sound patterns of language and this can be done through poetry, rhyme and in particualr nursery rhymes. Meek (1991) has said, 'Please teach children nursery rhymes, and the phonology will come, unnoticed, with fun' (p. 151).

4.4 Key concepts

There are two main ideas underpinning this chapter which are essential to a true understanding of the importance of rhyme and rhythm.

Listening to language

It is important to remember that we are talking about the sound system of language and so the activities which take place in the early years classroom will be oral. Very young children, by the time we encounter them in nursery, are well on the way to being very effective and efficient language users. They are able to hear differences in accent; they are able to identify rhyme and they are able to recognise patterns in language use. It is these skills and understandings which form the basis for future literacy learning and need to be built on and extended in the classroom. Children need to be given opportunities to listen to language – poems, stories, rhymes – and to identify patterns in both sound and structure. They will begin to identify words which rhyme and words which start with the same sound and they will also develop their feel for the structure of language as they hear examples of spoken language, book language and poetic language. They will also identify grammatical patterns, e.g. the structure of noun phrases or verb tenses and while not being able to give these labels will begin to know what is acceptable and what is not.

Playing with language

Even very young children enjoy playing with sounds, experimenting with their newly discovered vocalisation skills to see the different sounds they can make. As their language skills develop they play about with silly sentences and names. Children also begin to discover the patterns of language use, e.g. turn taking in conversations. We have all experienced the young child who tells you a completely non-funny joke; s/he may have understood the question and answer format of 'Knock knock, who's there?' but not the subtler play on words. That child is however playing with language and learning structural conventions.

In classroom activities children need to be given the opportunity to listen to and play with language. These are valuable learning times and can be fun too!

4.5 Rhyme and rhythm in play

Young children will naturally include rhyme and rhythm in their play and an effective early years teacher will create contexts and opportunities to exploit this delight in the sounds of language. It is true that much classroom work in this area will take place through focused activities but resources can be provided to encourage children to consider rhyme and rhythm in their play.

Listening centre

It has already been stressed that we cannot read to children too much, but the early years classroom is a busy place and adults are not always able to read when children wish. A listening centre provides a valuable source of spoken language through which the children can encounter all sorts of different language. Commercially-made tapes can be useful but often tapes made by the teacher or other adults can be more powerful. The listening centre can be available as a free-choice activity and can be used in many different ways. Here are just some ideas:

- Simple recordings of well-loved stories and rhymes. Choose ones with a strong rhythm, rhyme or structure and you will find that children will be joining in. Some you might use are:
  We're Going on a Bear Hunt
  This is the Bear
  Mig the Pig
  Mr Magnolia.
- Ask your friends and neighbours to make tapes for you so that children will hear a variety of voices and accents.
- Have recordings of common sounds and a set of pictures or photographs which the children have to match with the sound. You might record a telephone ringing, a car, a dog barking, a door shutting. While not specifically focusing on rhyme and rhythm, activities such as this help to develop children's listening skills, a vitally important aspect of language and literacy learning.
- To develop this in the reception class ask different people known to the children to speak and ask the children to match the voices to the photographs.

Tape recorders

These are not only valuable for listening activities, but also for allowing children to make their own recordings. Have one available in the classroom for the children to use during free-choice. This could be left unstructured so they will just play with sounds and enjoy listening to themselves, or it could be there with particular instructions, for example:

- Say a nursery rhyme onto the tape. These could be scribed later and a class nursery rhyme book made.
- Make a list of rhyming words. Chose a word for the day, e.g. cat, and every time children think of a word that rhymes they go and say it onto the tape. The tape can then be listened to as a whole class or group. The same could be done with words which start with the same sound.

Figure 4.1 Children at a listening centre

Role play

In the previous chapter we saw how role play can be used to develop children's understanding of, and response to, books and in the same way it can exploit their understanding of rhyme, building on their knowledge of nursery rhymes. Providing the appropriate props can stimulate children's imaginative play.

A nursery teacher put into the imaginative play area different objects relating to different nursery rhymes: a bowl, a dish, and a large furry spider on a string; a large clock and a toy mouse; a cuddly Humpty Dumpty, a wall made out of plastic interlocking building bricks, a crown and some toy horses, and a shepherd's crook and several toy sheep. As the children entered the area they firstly began to play quite randomly and then as they talked among themselves began to see the connections between the objects. Quite spontaneously they then began to act out nursery rhymes saying the rhymes out loud as they did so.

What was the purpose of this? Firstly, it caused the children to think and say nursery rhymes, and the link between children's knowledge of nursery rhymes and future literacy learning is well established (Goswami and Bryant 1991). Secondly, it invited the children to construct the 'stories' for themselves and to make the strong rhythmic language their own.

Musical instruments

Any consideration of rhythm in language cannot omit mention of music. Young children love making music and giving them free access to a range of instruments may give you a headache but will develop their own sense of rhyme and rhythm.

A reception class went out into the playground each carrying a musical instrument; there were drums, tambourines, triangles, cymbals, shakers, etc. They began by marching around the large space playing their instruments in time. Those who found it difficult were carried along by the others and it was surprising how quickly they fell into the rhythm. The children then began to say the nursery rhyme 'The Grand Old Duke of York' as they marched which helped them in maintaining the rhythm of their marching and emphasised the rhythm of the rhyme.

Figure 4.2 Children with musical instruments

4.6. Rhyme and rhythm in focused activities

Much work in this area can be done incidentally in the course of normal everyday routines:

- filling a space of five minutes with singing as many nursery rhymes as the children can think of;
- marching into the playground, garden or hall to the rhythm of a particular rhyme;
- thinking of words that rhyme with a given one;
- clapping the syllables of the children's names or of other long words.

There is also a place, however, for short activities with specific explicit teaching which will focus children's attention onto rhyme and rhythm. These can be done during circle time or with a small group during group time.

Shared writing

Shared writing is when the children behave as the authors of the text and the teacher or adult acts as secretary, scribing their ideas onto a large sheet of paper on an easel. It can serve several purposes and these will be outlined in detail in the following chapter.

Shared writing can also act as a useful focus for explicit teaching about rhyme through writing different versions of a well-known nursery rhyme, a process known as making innovation on a text.

The children in a reception class had made a large collage of Humpty Dumpty and the adult had written out the nursery rhyme in a small group time. A group of children read this together and as they read the adult drew their attention to the words that rhymed. The teacher then said, 'I wonder what would happen if we changed one of these words? Humpty Dumpty sat on a stool'. The children then read this with her and she then encouraged them to say the rest of the rhyme. When they got to the word 'fall' the children stopped and said, 'That's not right any more.' 'Why not?' asked the teacher and after some discussion the group came up with the fact that it didn't rhyme and they needed to think of a word that rhymed with 'stool'. Several suggestions were made: fool, pool, rule, cool, ghoul, jewel, mule. The teacher did not write them down because she wanted to concentrate on the oral rhyme and not confuse them by drawing attention to the different spelling patterns. After several false starts and with support the group decided on the line 'Humpty Dumpty fell into the pool' which the teacher wrote down. The discussion then continued until the rhyme was completed:

Humpty Dumpty sat on a stool.
Humpty Dumpty fell into the pool.
All the King's lifeguards
And all the King's swimmers
Couldn't make Humpty Dumpty float.

The children read it together and looked at the words 'stool' and 'pool' listening to the rhyme and identifying the written rime.

You may not think that rhyme has much literary merit but its composition provided many learning opportunities for the children. What had they done? They had:

- identified rhymes
- matched (almost!) the rhythmic pattern of the original rhyme
- explicitly discussed the rhyme and rhythm with each other and their teacher
- gone through the composition process, making choices of words, word order and structure
- seen their ideas written down and valued so they would begin to consider themselves as authors
- begun to make the connection between spoken and written language.

Later on, over a period of several weeks, other groups in the class wrote their own version of Humpty Dumpty. These were all written and illustrated in one class book which became a much read and well-loved part of the class book collection.

Syllables

Earlier in the chapter we saw how syllables provide the rhythm or beat of spoken language and focused work on syllables can help children to both hear and feel this.

Ideas could include:

- Clap the rhythm of children's names – one clap for each syllable, e.g. Di – ane (clap clap), Mar – gar – et (clap clap clap).
- Look for long words in the environment in books and through listening.
- Guess how many syllables a word has and then clap it as you say the word.
- Jump syllables. This game is a version of 'Grandma's Footsteps'. The adult stands at one end of the room or playground and the children at the other. The adult calls out a word and the children have to jump forward – one jump for each syllable.

Name game

The names of young children have great significance for them and anything which uses names as a focus is a powerful tool for learning. In this game, which is better played in a small group, think of words which rhyme with each child's name and make up phrases and rhymes about them. Some collected by a nursery class in this way included, 'late Kate, scary Mary, Wayne in the rain, Isobel fell in the well, see Lee and me'. It's a good idea if the adult has a rhyme for each name in the group as some names can tax even the most vivid imagination. If all else fails think of a word with the same number of syllables or starting with the same letter.

Odd one out

This is another game which can be played in a small group or as a whole class. The adult gives the children a list of about four or five words and they have to identify the odd one out, e.g. mug, rug, cup, bug. With very young children you are thinking about the sound of the rhyme and do not need to worry at this stage about words which sound the same but are spelt differently (homophones), e.g. chair, bear, fayre.

Oral cloze

A cloze procedure is when a teacher leaves out words from a text and the children use their syntactic and semantic knowledge to fill in the gaps. You may choose to omit every fifth word or you may choose to use it as a specific teaching focus and omit every adjective, every connective, or every preposition. In this context the focus is on rhyme and it is an oral rather than a written activity.

Choose a poem with a very strong rhyming pattern. Read it to the children leaving out alternate rhyming words and you will probably find that they will spontaneously fill the gaps.

Literature

There are many excellent children's books with both strong rhymes and rhythms. Use these as part of your normal reading diet and plan for rhyme to be a strong feature in the early years classroom. The Doctor Seuss books are an excellent example of strong rhyming stories which are great fun.

4.7. Rhyme and rhythm in the environment

We have already seen how the listening centre can be a useful resource for rhyme and rhythm, as can the use of musical instruments and rhyming books in the book corner.

There are other elements in the classroom environment which can be used to focus on rhyme and rhythm although it must be said that these will often serve as an extension and will begin to make the connection between spoken and written patterns of language.

Display

As you collect lists of rhyming words write them up and add to them as children find some more. You might want to make your displays in a visual form which will help the children remember the rhyming sound. For example:

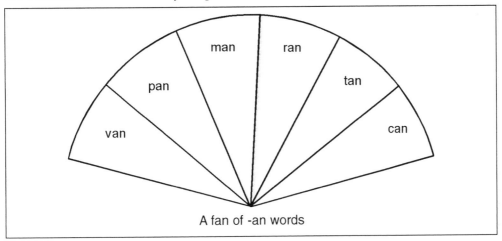

A fan of -an words

Figure 4.3 Rhyming words

Towards the end of the reception year children might well be ready to begin to focus on the different spelling patterns which represent a rhyming sound and word lists can be sorted to reflect differences.

Name cards

As you start to focus children's attention on print more specifically, use their name cards to highlight particular features. You could write each syllable in a different colour and use the name card as a prompt for those children who find it difficult to hear the rhythm.

Figure 4.4 Name cards

The outside environment

Asking the children to collect rhyming words that they hear in the playground, at home, or on television not only gives you a useful supply of words to 'play with' in school but also tunes children's ears in to the sounds of language. The Opies (1959) made a wonderful collection of playground rhymes and chants but an early years class can do just as well. The transcription of these rhymes can be a useful teaching resource.

Children also love advertising jingles and these can make a good starting point for consideration of rhyme and rhythm.

4.8. Planning, assessing and recording rhyme and rhythm

The Desirable Outcomes state that children will 'begin to associate sounds with patterns in rhymes, with syllables'. Before they can begin to do this we need to ensure that they can hear the sounds of language.

Many young children today have hearing problems and even those with very good hearing often have difficulty in listening to particular sounds. The world today is a noisy place and children are used to background noise which passes over their heads. Frequently children need to be trained in focused listening and many of the activities described in this chapter will support that training. Children will need to be able to listen both in story time and in discussion; they need to be able to articulate similarities and differences in sounds. They also need to be able to feel and describe the rhythm of language.

Planning in an early years setting needs to incorporate time for oral activities both as a whole class and for small groups. It needs to include opportunities in play and free-choice activities to consider the sound structures of language. Above all, it needs to make these opportunities and experiences fun so that children enjoy playing with language.

Much of our assessment for this aspect of children's learning will come through observation of normal classroom routines and activities. It is helpful to focus on a small group at a time so that observations can be specific. Questions you might ask yourself are:

- Can this child clap the syllables of her name?
- Can s/he identify the odd word out from a group of rhyming words?
- Can s/he clap and/or march in rhythm?
- Can s/he think of rhyming words?
- Can s/he identify rhyming words?
- Does s/he know many nursery rhymes?

Suffolk County Council (1996) has produced a booklet of many very useful ideas for activities to do with rhyme which gives some tasks for assessment. The first is a 'Rhyme Matching Task' where the child is shown some pictures on a page and a picture on a card. The picture on the card rhymes with one of the pictures on the page. 'I want you to put the card on top of the picture it rhymes with.' There are eight such pages of pictures. There is a similar task for alliteration (words beginning with the same sound).

Some teachers may find such tests useful but it is important to remember that young children, and indeed some adults, never perform to their full potential in a test situation and you need to ask yourself if it is necessary to carry out a test to discover the same information. Exactly the same resources could be put out on a free-choice table and the children's reaction observed. Observation is one of the most powerful tools the teacher of young children has and time for observation needs to be built into planning.

Awareness and knowledge of rhymes and rhythms of spoken language is a crucial aspect of early language and literacy learning. If a child is not able to hear and identify language rhymes and syllables s/he will not be ready to go to phonemic analysis. It is that which forms part of the focus of the next chapter.

5: Words and Letters

5.1. Defining terms

The Desirable Outcomes claim to 'cover important aspects of language development and provide the foundation for literacy'. It is significant therefore to note that they include a focus on the 'small shapes' (Barrs and Thomas 1991) of print. While taking account of this it is vital to keep literacy activities in the early years classroom grounded in those aspects of print which are relevant to young children. In their learning about words and letters children need to see them as part of the world of print which is used for specific purposes as well as for enjoyment by the authors they know and meet. Knowledge about words and letters gives children another strategy for the process of making sense of print; it is a means to an end and not an end in itself.

The Desirable Outcomes require that children 'begin to associate sounds ... with words and letters' and that they 'recognise their own names and some familiar words. They recognise letters of the alphabet by shape and sound.' This chapter considers how children can be helped to do this.

5.2. What children do

To young children their own name has much significance and they will frequently refer to the first letter of their name as 'my letter'. In the following chapter we will see how in their mark-making the first recognisable letters will usually be letters found in their name.

Children also recognise words they frequently see in the environment: most children will immediately know the word 'McDonald's' and Meek (1988) describes the little boy who calls the fox in *Rosie's Walk* 'MacDonald' because of the shape of his ears. This is a powerful example of the way in which children relate new experiences to what they already know and make sense of the new by comparing and contrasting it with the known. The popularity of programmes such as Sesame Street and the success of materials such as Letterland (Wendon 1986) show that children can come to a working knowledge of words and letters when they are placed within a meaningful context. The difficulty can come when children get stuck in the context and are not able to relate 'clever cat' to the abstract nature of letters.

A focus on words and letters can give children a language for talking about written language – what is known as a meta-language. This gives them control over their own use of language as they develop as readers and writers.

5.3 What the research says

The place of phonics teaching in language and literacy learning has been an issue of controversy for many years. There were those who argued that the whole was the most important and that sight vocabulary and knowledge of sound–symbol correspondence emerged from experiences of shared book reading (Smith 1978, Goodman and Goodman 1979). There were others who argued that literacy learning required a careful and cumulative introduction to the elements of written language: first letters, then words, then meaningful phrases or sentences and then stories and books (Gough 1972). Neither of these views really took into account the holistic nature of literacy processes (Stanovich 1980) nor the holistic way in which young children learn. As we read and write we draw on all areas of knowledge (about life, books, the structures and patterns of language, and sound–symbol representation). For many children those different knowledges come from their experiences of print and they are able to transfer this implicit knowledge to their reading and writing. Other children need these elements of the literacy process to be made more explicit to them and the current emphasis on specific focused teaching in literacy skills can only be a good thing (National Centre for Literacy 1997). The National Literacy Project's description of analysis at text, sentence and word level is both useful and helpful and reminds us of geographical analysis of the earth's surface. However, the deeper one delves the more important it becomes to continually return to the surface to keep both perspective and context in mind.

It appears that whenever there has been a concern about literacy standards phonic teaching is seen as the answer and that is certainly true of the current literacy initiative. Adams (1990) echoes this view when she says, 'Skilful reading depends uncompromisingly upon thorough familiarity with individual letters, words and frequent spelling patterns' (p. 115). This cannot be argued with but it must be put in the context of the meaning of the whole. A comparison can be drawn with learning to write; there is no point having beautiful handwriting if you have nothing to say and similarly there is no point having wonderful ideas if they are illegible when transcribed. There is no point in being able to identify all the component sounds of a word if you do not understand the meaning of the whole text. I am sure you will have had the same experience I have had when reading a particularly difficult text: I read each word articulating it in my head but when I got to the bottom of the page I realised that I had been thinking about going shopping later in the day and had not registered what the text was about. I had not really read it at all. Adams argues that both children and teachers must understand the purpose of activities and see how they fit into the whole; then, there can be no dispute about methodology for, 'written text has both form and function. To read, children must learn to deal with both and we must help them' (p. 123).

In the previous chapter the focus was on the phonological aspects of knowledge, i.e. the sound system of spoken English. We saw how the sound of English can be broken into words, syllables, and onset and rime. Spoken language can be broken further into phonemes which are the smallest unit of sound which can cause a change of meaning. 'Dog' is one word with one syllable; 'd' is the onset and 'og' is the rime. It has three phonemes d-o-g and changing any of these can cause a change in meaning, e.g. fog, dig or dot. Phonemic analysis is difficult; you might like to ask yourself how many phonemes there are in 'Wednesday' or 'soldier', remembering that phonemes refer to the sound of the language. It is generally thought that there are about 44 phonemes in Standard English. These 44 phonemes are represented by 26 letters, written symbols or graphemes and this is why written English is so complex.

For young children, analysis of words at phoneme level is not an easily accessible process (indeed you may find it difficult at first!) and it is more appropriate to concentrate on the onset and rime. This means that activities will look at rhyme and word families, as discussed in the last chapter, and also at initial sounds. Children also need to develop a vocabulary of words which they can recognise on sight and this will come through their experiences of print as they encounter 'key words' over and over again and have them pointed out to them. Repetition need not be boring and meaningless but can be great fun as the text of *The Cat in the Hat Comes Back* demonstrates.

5.4 Key concepts

In any work on words and letters three important principles need to be borne in mind:

1. The relationship between the 'big shapes' of the text and the 'small shapes' (Barrs and Thomas 1991). Any analysis of a text must keep the prime purpose of comprehension or composition in mind and so maintain the essential meaning of the text. Consideration of the small shapes is a way of facilitating access to the big shapes.
2. The starting point of any activity is more meaningful if it relates to something relevant to the child's experience and understanding. So playing with children's names and looking at print in the environment means that children are working with print with which they are familiar.
3. In order to be an effective reader, every child needs a vocabulary of words s/he is able to recognise immediately on sight, i.e. a sight vocabulary. Many of the key words children will meet as they share books with an adult both individually and as a group. As these are drawn to the children's attention they will begin to recognise them in other contexts and to begin the journey towards being an independent reader.

5.5 Words and letters in play

Playing with letter shapes

When learning about letters one of the significant concepts children need to grasp is that letters have a particular orientation. As they grow to learn the labels of particular objects they learn that a chair is a chair is a chair in whatever way it is positioned.

The differences in position make no difference to the identity of a chair but a 'b' is not a 'd' is not a 'p' is not a 'q'; position is a crucial factor in identification. However not all differences are so crucial; an 'a' is an 'A' is an α; the world of letters is confusing for the young child.

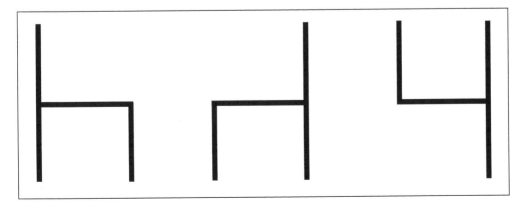

Figure 5.1 Chair in different positions

Free play with letter shapes is one way in which children can familiarise themselves with the forms of letters and with adult intervention talk about shape and pattern. Have letters made of wood, plastic, foam, sandpaper, or anything else you can think of. Encourage the children to sort, match, find the letters in their name, compare and describe.

Making letter shapes

Encourage children to make letter shapes out of a variety of materials – plasticine, play dough or clay. Let them write letters in wet sand, dry sand, finger paints, chalk or even in water on the playground. Often the feel of a letter shape will help children to recognise and remember them.

Physical Education (PE) and drama

Using particular words on flash cards as instructions can reinforce children's sight vocabulary. In PE you could hold up cards with prepositions – under, over, through, by. As you hold the card the children have to do what the card says in relation to their apparatus which could be a bench, a mat or a hoop.

In drama you could use nouns, adjectives or verbs to suggest particular movements. You might hold up cards with run, walk, hop, jump, etc. and children have to move in the way the card says. You could hold up cards with adjectives, e.g. happy, sad, angry, cross, and the children have to adopt the appropriate facial expressions.

5.6 Words and letters in focused activities

Word collections

Andy came to his nursery class one morning very excited as he had 'found a word'. His grandmother had bought a set of flash cards and Andy made the exciting discovery that the world was full of words. The teacher shared Andy's enthusiasm with the rest of the class who all decided to search for words themselves. A large display board in the classroom soon became covered with examples of words, cereal packets, labels, books, postcards, signs, etc. in which the children had been hunting for and finding words. To the untrained casual observer this looked an untidy collection of scraps of paper, but to the children and their teacher it was a powerful example of early literacy learning. What was the purpose of this activity? Firstly, the children were learning the concept of a word. In the previous chapter we saw how words are difficult to distinguish in spoken English but part of the skill of reading is to be able to identify word units in written English. Secondly, they were looking for, and at, print in the environment. This demonstrated to them the functions and purposes of print; they saw that print is part of life and not just that strange environment called nursery or school. Thirdly, they were talking about written language: about what it was doing and what it looked like. Written language became the topic of conversation in the classroom and as such the children's literacy awareness was raised.

Alphabet books and/or charts

Many early years classrooms structure learning through themes and this is an ideal opportunity for work on the alphabet. A topic on food can lead to an alphabet book of food: apple, butter, cake, doughnut, etc. Alphabet charts or books can be made of animals, occupations or flowers. If a whole alphabet is not possible then make an alphabet of adjectives or verbs. A topic on 'All About Me' led to a book 'I am angry, bored, clever, dozy', etc. A topic on movement could make an alphabet such as 'I act, bounce, crawl, dance', etc.

Literacy walks

The role of print in the environment is important to children's literacy learning. Take a small group for a walk around the immediate local environment, encouraging the children to look for examples of written language. As the children identify an example read to them what it says, pointing if possible to the words as you read. Ask the children why that print is there – is it telling people something? warning them? inviting them in? etc. A knowledge of the purposes and functions of print can make reading more relevant for the children and seeing words within a context can help to build a sight vocabulary.

Slightly older children could go on a literacy walk to look for examples of particular words. 'How many times do you think we will find the word "the" on this noticeboard?'

Object collections

A common activity in early years classrooms is to collect objects beginning with a particular sound. As someone who has spent many a hurried morning searching for an object starting with 'r' that nobody else will have thought of, I can vouch for the efficacy of this strategy! Be adventurous in the way in which you display these and remember that in order to make the sound–symbol relationship obvious the initial

Figure 5.2 'g' picture

letter needs to be clear. Displays could include a basket of 'b' objects, an umbrella of 'u' objects, a mountain of 'm' objects, a dinosaur of 'd' objects, a sandwich of 's' things or a garage in a garden as in Figure 5.2.

Pelmanism

This game is useful for practising sight vocabulary. On small cards write the common words that children are beginning to recognise, e.g. the, and, is, of, but, in. Write each word on two cards. Spread the cards out upside down on a table in a regular pattern. The children then take it in turns to turn over two cards. If they turn over a pair they have to read the word and are then able to keep the cards.

You can vary the difficulty of this game by the number of words you use; you may have sixteen cards with only two words or you may have sixteen cards with eight words.

Group cloze procedure

Cloze procedure is when you omit words from a text; this may be done randomly leaving out every fifth or tenth word or it may be done to focus attention on a particular word class, e.g. verbs or adjectives. Here we are using it to focus attention on those common words which have no meaning in their own right.

On a large sheet of paper write out a nursery rhyme well known to the children but leave out one particular word, e.g.:

Humpty Dumpty sat on ____ wall.
Humpty Dumpty had a great fall.
All ____ King's horses and
All ____ King's men,
Couldn't put Humpty together again.

Clip this onto an easel and gather a small group of children around you. Have a selection of cards on which you have different words written

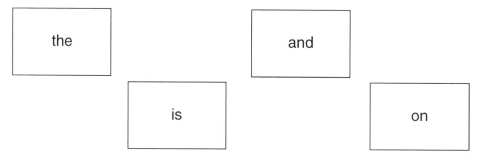

Make sure the cards are all the same size even though the words are not. Say the nursery rhyme with the children and then draw their attention to the printed version. Read it together and you will probably find the children read even the missing word. Draw their attention to this, 'Oh dear, one of the words has fallen off. Let's see if we can fill in the gap. Here are some words, I wonder if any of them will fit'. Ask a child to choose one of the words on the card and stick it into the gap. On each occasion re-read the line drawing particular attention to the focus word.

Games with names

Write each child's name on a card. Gather a small group around you and hold up the name cards in turn seeing if they can recognise their own name.

Once the children are familiar with their written names draw their attention to the first letter. Put those whose names begin with the same letter together. Have large cards with the appropriate letters on and ask the children to put their name cards on 'their letter'. Give each child a bag or box and ask them to collect objects which start with their letter. Match their names with an alphabet chart and begin to talk about alphabetical order. Stand the children in order holding their name cards. Let the children paint self-portraits and make a frame of letter shapes.

5.7 Words and letters in the environment

Display

In creating a literate environment within the classroom you can draw children's attention to particular words or letters in several ways. As you focus on a particular letter each week, making collections of words starting with that letter, keep previous collections and put them into a class dictionary. Children will enjoy looking back and remembering which object they brought.

Label objects around the room using complete sentences and highlighting the focus word, e.g.

- Shut the *door.*
- Look through the *window.*
- The puzzles go in the *cupboard.*

Occasionally take all the labels off and ask the children to stick them back in the right places. Or put them in the wrong place and ask the children to sort them out for you.

Book corner

From time to time create a feature of alphabet books in the book corner. Encourage children to read them in silent reading time, and read them to the children at story time. Include alphabet books the children have made themselves. Put on the wall as many different alphabets or individual letters as you can find – wrapping paper is often a useful source for this. An alternative idea is to choose books which match your letter of the week. If you are thinking about 'b' then display all the bear books you have; if the letter is 't' then make stories about *Titch* (Pat Hutchins) your focus.

Imaginative play

Provide the children with resources which all begin with the same letter – monsters, masks, machines, merry-go-round, map, music, etc. Let the children play freely with these resources and then ask them to tell you the story of their 'play'. 'Have you noticed anything the same about all these things?'

Writing corner

In Chapter 6 we will talk about setting up a writing corner in the classroom where children can freely write in their play. As children become familiar with words and letters and begin to develop a sight vocabulary, start to create a word bank in the writing area. Have lists of common words and pictures and names of objects in pockets on the wall. These can become available to children to use as resources in their mark-making as are the pencils, pens and paper. Put no pressure on the children at all; as they become more aware of and familiar with the conventions of print they will begin to include them in their writing.

5.8 Planning, assessing and recording

It is all too easy when assessing children's knowledge of sound and shape of letters to consider that a simple checklist is enough. You list all the letters and tick them off when a child knows them. You might even want to work with each child individually and work down the list of letters checking their recognition. Beware of this! You will find that it does not give you a true picture of children's knowledge and understanding, but a rather impoverished, sterile list.

There is a large body of research which gives a picture of the vast range of knowledge about literacy which young children have (e.g. Heath 1983, Hall 1987). Stierer *et. al.* (1993) say,

> young children will ... have spent a lot of time studying literacy-based elements in their environment and observing people using literacy, and that they will have put some powerful effort into unravelling the phenomena of reading and writing' (p. 5).

In our assessment we need to observe that process and see how much children are using their knowledge and understanding in a variety of contexts. Some of the questions you might ask yourself include:

- Is s/he beginning to use recognisable letter shapes in his/her mark-making?
- Does s/he recognise individual words when sharing books with adults?
- Does s/he recognise letter shapes in a variety of contexts and is s/he able to generalise that knowledge, i.e. s/he knows an R when it is on its side, upside down, in upper and lower case and in a variety of different scripts?
- When s/she reads, does what s/he says approximate to the text and is there a one-to-one correspondence between spoken and written word?
- Does s/he use initial letters as a clue for identifying words?
- Are there some words s/he recognises on sight when reading and is beginning to use in his/her writing?
- Does s/he identify letters in words in both books and environmental print?

The answer to these questions will emerge from regular frequent observations which will note children's behaviours as readers and writers and their growing familiarity and confidence with the conventions of print. The information gained from these observations will form the basis for planning of future activities. Contexts and opportunities need to be created in which authentic experiences with print enable children to draw on and extend their knowledge of words and letters.

6: Mark-making and Writing

6.1 Defining terms

We use the Desirable Outcomes statement as a definition of what we mean by Early Writing, 'In their writing they use pictures, symbols, familiar words and letters, to communicate meaning, showing awareness of some of the different purposes of writing' (p. 3).

Children's first attempts at writing show little evidence of the conventions of print. Many children will accompany their mark-making, however, with comments which show that they are using what they know to communicate meaning. For example, the child might say, 'This is a letter for Grandpa' or 'Here is my shopping list'. For the purposes of this chapter we have used the term 'writing' to encompass the wide range of marks children make as they engage in writer-like behaviour.

We consider the compositional and transcriptional elements of writing and the links between writing and speech, laying emphasis on the importance of talking about and demonstrating the writing process.

6.2 What children do

A useful way to discuss writing is to think of it as having two aspects, composition and transcription. In a scenario described by Frank Smith (1982) the author is dictating to his/her secretary; the author is composing the text and the secretary is transcribing it. They are both writing but they are concerned with different things. The author, composing, concerns him/herself with getting ideas, choosing words, and organising language so that it communicates the intended message. The secretary, transcribing, will be engaged in the physical act of writing, paying attention to the details of script which effectively records what the author dictates. S/he will be concerned with aspects of punctuation, capitalisation, spelling, and legibility. Both are important, but it is transcription which serves composition.

The Desirable Outcomes incorporate both transcription, 'use pictures, symbols, familiar words and letters' and composition, 'to communicate meaning', because, of course, we want children to develop in both aspects.

Transcription

When children arrive in the early years setting they will bring with them a wide range of knowledge and experience relating to print and letters. Many will already be able to write their own names and recognise and produce some letters. There is much to learn. There are 52 letter signs (26 upper case and 26 lower case), plus letter variations for 'a' and 'g', plus punctuation signs, 'a large amount of discrimination learning for any child' (Clay 1975, p. 42). Most children, keen to learn about writing, write long before they have mastered all these. Their writing does not look like ours, of course, in much the same way as their first words do not sound like ours. Sadly, some 'adults seem to be reluctant to bother with a jumbled set of letters in early writing or a story that has been written from right to left. They prefer not to read what the child is saying until he presents it in a easily read form' (p. 16). If this is the case then how it contrasts with the adult's response to early speech. We saw in Chapter 1, and will see again in Chapter 7, that adults work hard at using surrounding information to interpret the child's first sounds, so why not put as much effort into interpreting their first attempts at writing?

Also in Chapter 1 we categorised children's talk as moving through pre-communicative speech (where sounds are not like adult speech and communication or understanding is limited to those around the child) to transitional speech (where enough sounds are recognisable that other adults can interpret with use of context) and to conventional speech (where the child's talk is much like the adult's and easily understood). We have used the terms pre-communicative, transitional and conventional because they help us to show you that early writing development has links with the development of speech.

Pre-communicative writing
Stacey read this writing to her teacher, 'Miss Jackson is very brave to catch a lion'.

Figure 6.1 Pre-communicative writing

Transitional writing
One of the items on this shopping list is 'wrapping paper'.

Figure 6.2 Transitional writing

Conventional writing
Figure 6.3, a thank you letter, although not entirely correct, is easily read. It will not surprise you that the key conditions which foster talk will also contribute to fostering writing. Talk is fostered when the learner is invited into the talking community, where talk is an act of meaningful communication, and where the learner receives many models of talk. Writing is fostered when the learner is invited into the writing community, where writing is an act of meaningful communication, and where the learner receives many models of writing. Given these conditions we would expect that children, as in learning to talk, would actively reach out to writing and engage in and initiate writing activity. Many do just this as is evidenced in many collections of early writing.

One of the earliest lessons a child has to learn concerning writing is that what they say can be written down, and the practice of scribing for young children is based on this understanding. When you take dictation from a young child, perhaps to accompany a picture or photograph, make sure that you write down exactly what the child wants you

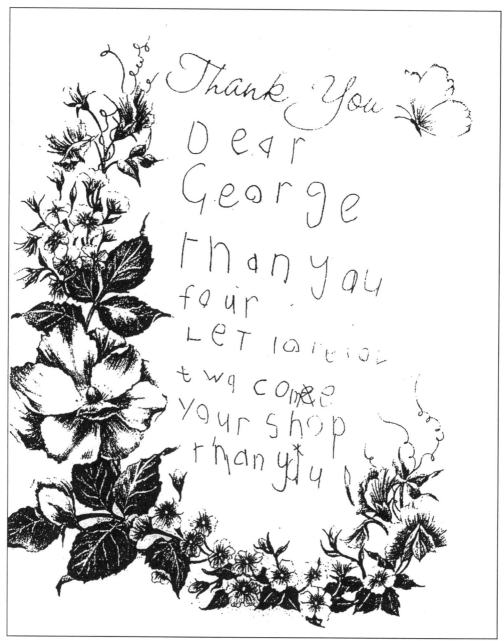

Figure 6.3 Conventional writing

to write because you may want to use the print for a mini-reading lesson. Should you ask the child to read it back to you s/he will, of course, be relying heavily on memory. The child should be seeing what s/he says. Any differences between spoken text and scribed text should be negotiated and understood by the child. There will be negotiations because you will, as well as showing the child that you can write down what s/he says, be showing the child that writing differs from speech.

The way we say things in writing is not the same as recording what we would say 'face-to-face'. Written language is more precise, to cope with the fact that the reader is distanced from the writer by time and/or space. If you have worked closely with young children you will know how much easier it is to scribe for a child who can talk like a book. Once again we see the importance of shared reading, not to make our work easier, I hasten to add, but to teach the child that the language of print is different from the language of speech. How complicated. Children have to learn that what they say can be written down but they also have to learn that writing is not simply speech written down.

We would like you to recognise some of the complexity of learning to write. Try listening to a short extract on the radio; Radio 4 is likely to give you some suitable material. Listen for about two minutes and then write a summary of what you heard using the hand you don't usually use to write.

Reflect on the experience, thinking about and if possible discussing with a colleague questions such as:

- What were you aware of? How did it feel?
- What did you do when you didn't know the spelling?
- What other problems did you encounter? How did you cope?
- Do early writers share these feelings? In what ways is the task of writing different for them?

Do you get some idea of the challenges children face? How can we help them? Barrs *et al.* say,

> Most of the problems connected with learning to 'write' are problems to do with transcription and most approaches to teaching writing have been ways of dealing with transcription. There are two main ways in which teachers now help children who are learning to write: a) by making transcription easier and b) by encouraging independence' (1988, p. 30).

By scribing and by recording their stories on tape we are helping the child to produce written text without the physical challenges of transcription. The more ways we can do this the better. Why not invite a parent in to type on the word processor? Make books with children, use the children's experiences to make newspapers and magazines, etc.

In addition to this encourage children to write themselves. If they see you doing so much writing and enjoying it, and if you respond positively to their attempts, then they will want to do it themselves. Quite often very young children will surprise us with the knowledge of different forms of writing which they demonstrate when they are given the chance. So look for ways of providing children with the confidence and opportunity to show you what they know by providing them with contexts for writing which as well as developing their transcription skills give attention to composition and form.

Spelling

You will find much has been written about spelling, and among the names you should look for are Peters (1985) and Torbe (1977). Be sure that what you read acknowledges the recent developments in our knowledge of the English writing system, in particular the work carried out regarding what is known as developmental spelling. Here is a transcript of Joanne and Clare working out how to spell 'video':

J: I wanted video, video, video ...
C: I know it ... I know how to spell video. I say vid-de-o and then I can get the word ... that's what I do. Vid-de-o. Vid ... ah d have you done a d?... then de... vid-de-vid
J: Which way does d go?
C: Vid-de-o vid video
J: Is that video?
C: I think this is video
J: I'll ask Miss.

Clare uses her knowledge of the relationships between sound and symbol as she works out how to spell a word which, as yet, is not in her sight vocabulary.

It is at this stage in early writing when adults are charmed by children's often idiosyncratic spellings in much the same way as they are charmed by children's early speech productions. What do you think this writing of Mark's says?

Figure 6.4 'Iguana' writing

It says 'This is a iguana'. Such confidence and willingness to have a go is admirable. 'Children who have a good general understanding of sound–symbol relationship, even if they do not spell well at the moment, are, as Margaret Peters says, 'well on their way' to becoming good spellers' (Torbe 1977, p. 46).

Later, both Clare and Mark will learn that actually very many words are not spelt according to how they sound but how they look. The texts you read concerning spelling will emphasise the visual aspect of spelling. Torbe says that a poor speller generally has weak visual memory and/or weak auditory analysis. So, for very young children activities which develop their abilities to discriminate visually and auditorily are essential.

Handwriting

Sassoon (1990) shows us that handwriting is a taught skill and that children must learn the correct letter formation so that they develop a style that is comfortable, fluent and legible. At first there appears to be conflict between this and the move towards children experimenting and writing independently. When do you teach young children how to form letters? We wish we could give you an easy answer to this, but like everything else in teaching and learning it depends. It depends on the child's state of knowledge about letters, it depends on the child's manual dexterity, it depends on the child's understanding of the task.

We think you should read what Charles Cripps has to say about both handwriting and spelling, which he sees being developed together. In *Joining the ABC* (1992) Charles Cripps and Robin Cox advocate the teaching of a joined hand from the beginning because it helps children acquire the concept of a word. It also means that, because the letters join, correct letter formation and letter-strings (patterns within words) become habitual. Two key elements of their work, in relation to very young children, are that 'joining' follows letter awareness and that writing from memory is paramount. The kind of activities which foster pencil control are those commonly found in the early years art and craft curriculum.

> It is also important that pattern work continues throughout the children's development and is not seen simply as a stage in a continuum which is to be forgotten once mastered .... Probably the best way to increase children's patterning ability as well as motor control is through art and craft (1992).

Also supportive of handwriting development are ball games, cutting and sticking, construction, jigsaw puzzles, toys and games, finger rhymes, moulding (e.g. clay, plasticine, dough), finger painting, pencil play.

For children in the early years, approaches to handwriting and spelling will focus on their fascination with letters, especially those in their own names. They will learn the names of letters in much the same way as they learn the names of everyday objects, through using and talking about them. Give them opportunities to see you writing in a variety of different scripts and talking about it as you do so.

Composition

Young children are composing all the time, as we saw in the chapter on story. Provided this skill is nurtured and encouraged it can be used to move children towards greater writer-like behaviour. We need to consider what it is that writers actually do when they are composing. They bring knowledge to their composition:

- knowledge about the topic
- knowledge about language.

They bring expectations to their composition:

- expectations relating to the purpose of the work
- expectations relating to the audiences for their work.

They bring experience to their composition:

- experience of previous compositions
- experience of reading the work of other authors.

All of this they bring to their writing. It is easy to extrapolate from this some key principles regarding the tasks we offer children (Fig. 6.5).

CHILDREN NEED:	WHAT WE DO:
to know about the topic	Provide first-hand experiences
	Recognise existing experiences and knowledge
to know about language **to know about writing**	Talk about language/play with language Talk about writing Provide lots of opportunities for children to write
	Write in front of children, for a variety of purposes and audiences
to know about authors	Share the work of authors: • by providing key texts written for children • by talking about the author and authorship
to know why they are writing	Provide many reasons for children to write: a) to entertain b) to persuade c) to express feelings d) to inform e) to request f) to instruct
	Help children find appropriate forms for above, e.g. a) a story b) an advert c) a card d) a newspaper e) a letter f) a recipe
to know who they are writing to	Providing audiences for above, e.g. a) for a teddy b) for a class magazine c) for a family member d) for parents e) for a friend f) for older children

Figure 6.5 Developing writers

Ways of meeting the children's needs as outlined will be found in the surrounding text, but we want to pick up on one key issue, that of talking about writing, authors and their work. Meek (1988) says that if we want to see what lessons children learn from their reading then we should look to their writing. If we want children to write imaginatively then we should provide models from authors who write with imagination. If we want children to write using language creatively then we should read to them from the work of authors with the ability to play with words. If we want children to write to instruct then we should share instruction manuals with them. And we do want children to learn to write in many different forms and for many different purposes so the texts we choose to share with children must give them models and concepts which provide them with a firm foundation for the development of their own compositional skills.

And when we have provided children with access to these texts, and the chapter on reading talks more about choosing texts, we should occasionally use them so that the writing process can be made explicit, so that children come to see the nature of the task, in particular what writing is good for. Children need to learn about print and this learning revolves around these key questions:

- What kind of text is it? Because we are not only talking about stories and books. We are taking the widest definition of text to include environmental texts such as adverts, signs, labels.
- Who wrote it? Because children need to know that texts are created and not a product of the natural world. Children are surrounded by print and it is easy to see how they might regard it as they regard trees, for example.
- Who did s/he write it for? Because behind all texts is an imagined audience. Road signs are for drivers, greetings cards are for friends and family, etc.
- Why did s/he write it? Because all authors have something they want to achieve with written text. The authors of most junk mail want us to buy something and the author of the weather report wants to satisfy our desire to know if it will rain or shine.

We have something we would like you to try the next time you are working with a group of preschool children. We and other colleagues have come to call this activity 'The Prop Bag' because the only resource, or prop, you need is a selection of texts which you can collect from your own home. We put things such as bus tickets, driving licence, cheque book, till receipt, shopping list, etc. into a 'feely' bag and invited children to come and pick an item and then talk about it. Our prompting questions were as above: what is it, who wrote it, who for and why? We think, like us, you will be surprised at the children's responses. Some children knew exactly what a till receipt was for and they helped us help those children who had clearly never thought about it before. On one occasion a child pointed out that there was a telephone number on the receipt so that we could ring up and complain if we wanted to. Shame on us that we had never noticed this!

You might like to read the actual conversation:

T: What's this then?
C1:   Tescos Miss
C2:   It's a ... ticket

C1:   Receipt
T: What does it tell us?
All C: What to buy
C1:   Is it a receipt?
T: It tells us all the things to buy, and what else does it tell us?
C1:   Thank you for shopping at Tescos
T: Have another look. Come round here Hayley
C2:   Tells you how much
T: Tells you how much
T: Oh that's kind isn't it – Thank you for
          shopping at Tescos – down there
C1:   And it tells you their phone number
T: It hasn't got the phone number on has it?
C3:   Yeah – at the bottom
T: So it has! Is there anything else on there?
          ... unclear ... Has it got the date on?
C2:   No. I don't think so
C3:   My mum used to work at Tescos
C2:   My mum does
T: Do you only get these at Tescos?
All C: No. You get them at every shop
C1:   Not the sweet shop
C3:   Yeah, some sweet shops
C2:   Martins you get one from
T: What actually makes one then?
All C: A till ... a machine ...
T: When it's all on the till, do you know what it's called
C2:   A roll.

This transcript was part of a larger transcript where children talked about wrapping paper, birthday cards, newspapers, etc., because they were going to set up a newsagent's shop in their setting. This was an ideal context for giving children the opportunity to write in a range of forms for a variety of purposes and audiences.

Figure 6.6 shows examples of some of their work.

The challenge to the adults in the early years setting is to provide children with a variety of reasons to write and readers to write for, so how about setting up a newsagent's shop in your setting? You will be giving the children reasons to write, providing models for writing, and when the children play there you will be able to encourage them to think about function, purpose and audience. Having provided the context you will also need to think about supporting children in the process of writing.

The writing process

The best way to conceptualise the writing process is to write yourself. Think about the last piece of writing that was important to you and see how much of the following you recognise. We are following the lead of Wray and Medwell (1994) by using our own experience to focus on aspects of the writing process.

We made:

Remember.

Miss Jo nns

MSSDYSON

mss Geer / Mss Jug s

Shopping Lists

get well soon

Greetings Cards

My little Pone

Video Covers.

Figure 6.6 Newsagents

In the writing of this text:

- Margaret talked with the publishers who had the idea that a book like this was needed. They helped with an outline plan, i.e. putting Desirable Outcomes into practice. They also identified the potential audience.
- We agreed broad framework of content, style and responsibility.
- Individually we brainstormed each chapter, made an outline plan, began the first draft, referred to other texts and talked to other people, re-read, modified and re-arranged text and produced a first draft. We read each other's drafts and acted as response partners. There was then more editing for greater clarity and coherence and the final draft was assembled on disk for final joint editing. The manuscript was sent to the publishers who reviewed it. There was more modification relating to the publishers' note; the proofs were read and finalised; the book was published and you bought it. Not all work proceeds to publication, of course, and every author has his/her individual way of tackling the task. However, it is possible to identify a model of the writing process which looks something like this:

Stage 1 – decision making
Stage 2 – planning
Stage 3 – drafting
Stage 4 – redrafting
Stage 5 – re-reading
Stage 6 – proofreading.

These stages are identified in the National Curriculum as being important in the writing process. Not all writing proceeds in a linear fashion through these stages, for example, decisions are made throughout, but most writing contains the above elements and these illustrate clearly that writers often have to monitor (re-read) and modify (redraft) their work. Authors accept that their first brainstorm of ideas will go through a process of change before their work is suitable for its intended audience. Here we reach a possible dilemma in relation to young children. Our experience of young children writing shows that very often first is best, and there is an understandable reluctance in the early years field to the suggestion that a child should rewrite their work.

> It is striking to note how cautious Bereiter and Scardamalia are about primary children redrafting their writing. They note that children find their first drafts 'highly salient' and that exhortations to redraft can lead to superficial tinkering which may threaten to diminish the overall effectiveness of the text (Wray and Medwell 1994, p. 108).

If the 'exhortation to redraft' is inappropriate for primary children, how much more so would it be for preschool children who are just beginning to experiment with writing. But, we are not suggesting that you exhort your children to redraft by re-writing, more that you provide the option. The decision has to be in the hands of the writer who sees that s/he needs to make his/her message clearer to the reader. What we are suggesting is that you create an environment where children know that this is what writers do. Writers plan, do, and review.

Children can be encouraged to plan by talking their writing through, perhaps as a small group with an adult scribing or feeding back their thinking. This kind of support is usually well used in many early years settings and, where it mirrors the writing process described above, becomes a form of oral drafting. Less widely used, in our experience, is planning and drafting through modelling.

Here you can see children in a reception class using Lego to plan a map showing other children (audience) how to get from school to the shops (purpose). The Lego provides the children with a medium through which they draft their work. They can change their ideas and modify them in response to new information and new ideas. These children changed their ideas in response to comments made by their friends and it was possible to see the detail grow as children made sure that their friends would be able to find the shops. The end product reflected this rehearsal and collaboration.

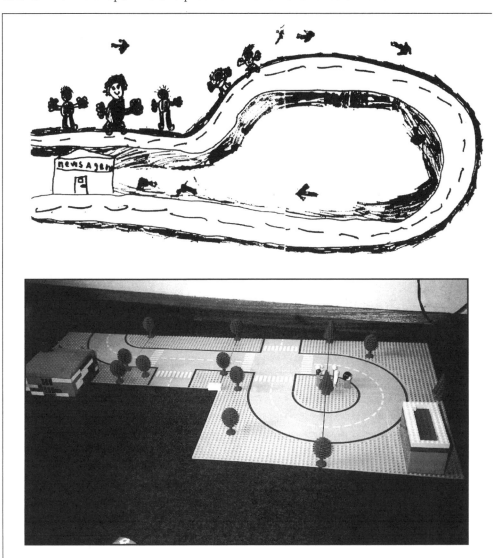

Figure 6.7 Lego and drawn map

This technique of modelling, along with oral planning and drafting, applies equally well to story and other forms of writing where it acts as a rehearsal for the final product.

In addition to finding ways for children to plan and review their writing children need to see the process in action. Shared writing is one way for an adult to model the writing process, and we say more about this later. When you write with and for children, voice what it is that you do when you compose, so that when the children reach the point when they have a clear sense of purpose and audience and when they see the need for change, they feel that this is what we expect of them, not that we expect them to get it right first time.

6.3 What the research says

The 1980s saw a surge of interest in young children's early independent reading and writing-like behaviours. Dame Marie Clay is one of the many researchers who have collected examples of young children's independent writing in order to identify features of development in writing. She is a 'kid watcher', a phrase coined by Yetta Goodman (1985) who was also a 'kid watcher'. This generation of observers of children has given us many insights into children's learning and literacy development, insights which have impacted on the early years classrooms where the term 'emergent literacy' is now embedded.

The Desirable Outcomes state that 'In their writing they use pictures, symbols, familiar words and letters, to communicate meaning, showing some awareness of the different purposes of writing' (p. 3). Temple *et al.* (1988) provide a very interesting account of 'how writing systems are organised' (p. 11) where we can see how pictures and symbols were the precursors of the script we use today. As children explore and experiment with writing they 'appear to be trying to discover and manipulate principles that can make their productions look like writing' (Temple *et al.* 1988, p. 26). Temple *et al.* used the work of M. Clay and we will follow this lead asking you to keep the Desirable Outcomes in mind and remember that writing here includes pictures and symbols.

Clay presents an impressive collection of early writing where there is evidence that

> the first things learnt will be gross approximations which later become refined: weird letter forms, invented words, make-believe sentences. Such creative efforts suggest that the child is reaching out towards the principles of written language and any instruction should encourage him to continue doing this (1975, p. 15).

Clay identified certain principles that children know about writing and which they demonstrate in their own writing. We recommend that you look for similar examples in your own setting.

Principles that children know about writing

The recurring principle
Where the child is learning that writing is about repeating the marks. This repetition can often be found in their drawings where they develop 'schema' for people and houses.

The directional principle
Where the child is learning that writing in English goes from left to right and makes a return sweep to the left in order to proceed from the top to the bottom of the page.

The generating principle
Where the child uses the elements of what s/he knows in order to make new statements. S/he learns that 'long statements are generated from a limited number of symbols' (Clay 1975, p. 27).

The inventory principle
Where the child 'takes stock' of his/her own repertoire of symbols, letters, and words. Lists are common features of this principle where children seem to be trying to organise their knowledge.

The flexibility principle
Where the child learns to make new letters out of those s/he knows and where they turn letters round, decorate them, write in different directions, etc. They learn what features make a letter different from another and what is acceptable in our system.

Children writing in this way are learning to differentiate letters, that writing consists of repeating and rearranging letters in a variety of combinations, and that it proceeds in a set way across and down the page. Similar principles are observed when children learn about spaces between words, punctuation, abbreviation, capitalisation and page layout. They learn through trying to solve the problem, 'What makes writing writing?'

Clay's work here is concerned with what Wray and Medwell (1991) call the mechanical aspects of writing and she reminds us that there are two perspectives here, the psychological perspective and the social psychological perspective. The first, similar to that of Clay, is illustrated by the work of Ferreiro and Teberosky (1983), who studied children's concepts about print and how they developed. Like Clay they saw children's writing development as a series of speculations and hypotheses about writing. Central to their work is the concept that children need to understand the difference between drawing and writing.

Richard, having '4' on his page and not 'four', told me that he wrote letters and drew numbers:

R: I've even put the number instead of writing the number.
Me: You have, yes, that's quicker still.
R: I've just drawn the number.
Me: What could you have done instead then?
R: I could have written the numbers.
Me: You could have written it. Is that drawing it? That's not writing the number ... that's drawing the number is it?
R: Yep!

Clearly Richard knew a lot about writing and I wish I'd had the presence of mind to ask him about the difference between drawing and writing. Perhaps you could ask the children you meet and see what interesting answers you get! Ferreiro and Teberosky found that children at a particular level of understanding thought that words represented objects, like drawings, the only difference being that they did not look like them. Later they learn that words are linked to speech.

Harste *et al.* (1984) hold a social psychological perspective, and are more concerned about children's understanding of literacy. They would not be able to discover what they think important, that children negotiate, take risks, have intentions and make decisions, from simply looking at samples of writing. They would want to know about the context in which it was written, because they consider the social dimension to be as influential in writing as it is in speech. Why the children wrote it, for whom, and under what circumstances are therefore of equal importance, and this can only be discovered by being involved with the child as s/he writes, by listening to and observing the child at work.

Research into writing will often emphasise transcription over composition or vice versa. Yetta Goodman (1990, p. 135) integrates these and puts them in the context of children's experiences as talkers, readers and writers. Goodman, working with two- to six-year-olds since 1973, suggests that the act of literacy learning is an act of 'learning how to mean' and that children's development of literacy has its roots in the encounters with literacy that the child has. She identifies three major roots and we summarise them here.

Functions and forms of literacy

Children respond to logos, symbols, and signs in their environment. They are introduced to 'connected discourse' when they share books, magazines, comics, etc. They learn about the different forms of literature, and the functions they fulfil, by taking part in 'meaningful literacy events'.

Using oral language about written language

'Children and other members of society talk about the literacy events in which they participate' (p. 137).

Conscious knowledge about literacy

Where written language is something of interest, something to talk about. Take Richard, above, he had developed 'conscious knowledge about written language' at home.

From the work of these researchers we can conclude that the role of the early years practitioner is to engage young children in meaningful literacy events, to talk about them, to encourage children as independent writers and then to sample their writing to see what principles s/he is generalising about print. They also, of course, need to show children how they write and we will talk about this later when we talk about shared writing

6.4 Key concepts

At the forefront of our thinking about writing is the concept that it is an act of communication, where the writer has something to say to the reader. Many young writers know this; they will have been invited by their parents to make shopping lists, send cards to family, write letters to Father Christmas, send postcards, leave notes, and many other literacy events. Some children have yet to learn this and it will be important for them to engage in similar experiences in the early years setting. It will be important for all children to continue meaningful encounters with literacy events.

Children learn to speak before they learn to read and write and what they know about and can do with talk will be a strong supporter of their learning to read and write. Remember that oracy and literacy are linked. Children learn from other people, experience of sharing texts written by others gives children an insight into the writing process. Talking about writing both as a reader and as a writer is important for children's developing understanding and knowledge about writing.

What do we need to do? We need to:

- place meaning at the forefront of learning about written language. The child is the meaning maker when s/he writes, and s/he needs to be supported in making choices which convey his/her messages effectively to the reader.
- accept the fact that development takes place on many fronts at the same time. A child writing a recipe will be learning about the creative aspects of writing (e.g. how to communicate what to do), the structural aspects of writing (how to organise it), and the conventional aspects of writing (e.g. how you spell it). Development is not linear but there are common features in children's early attempts at writing.
- understand the importance of experimentation and risk-taking in the process of learning to write. When children are encouraged to write even though they have limited ability as transcribers, they are capable of producing continuous and independent texts. Their compositional skills are in advance of their transcriptional skills and their transcriptional immaturities need to be seen as evidence of learning, not mistakes.
- support children's experiments. We need to find ways in which we can support without discouraging children from writing independently. We can let them see us write and write with them. We can learn from their writing so that we can help them move forward.
- recognise the importance of giving writers audiences for their writing. Writers need readers who respond to their messages.
- provide demonstrations of what it is to be a writer. Adults can demonstrate the kinds of choices they make when they are writing: what they say; how they present it; what they do about spelling; what they do if they want to change it.

The adult in the early years setting has two major functions to fulfil concerning children's development as writers: s/he provides contexts for the children's writing and makes responses to their writing. Make sure that the contexts you provide include opportunities for children to write for a range of purposes in a variety of forms. Make sure also that your responses are to both what has been said and how it has been said.

6.5 Writing in play

The adult in the early years setting should review the activity of the setting in terms of the opportunities it offers for children to explore writing. Just as a telephone encourages talk, a note pad and pen encourages writing, as children are introduced to the idea of taking messages from the telephone. Pencil and paper should be easily available so that it can be drawn into children's play as often as is possible. Think of the writing props that might be included in the imaginary play area. A cafe needs menus, posters, price lists, order pads, etc. A space ship needs manuals, control labels, rotas, instructions, danger signs, log books, etc. It is worth spending some time making a list of possibilities for the areas you are planning.

A key feature of the writing environment is the writing area and we want to spend the rest of this section considering how this might be arranged and used.

The writing area

A writing area is a place where children can go, at will, to explore different forms of writing. A writing area becomes a central resource where materials can be organised and managed sensibly and at the same time provide ease of access. A writing area shows that writing is important and worthwhile, it demonstrates to the children and to visitors that the institution values literacy.

How to set up a writing area

First identify the position of the proposed writing area. The space can vary from a fairly large corner to a small table; both benefit from being in a quiet spot away from activities which call for a high level of movement. If it is a small area it should allow two children to work together collaboratively. All writing areas benefit from a display area such as a wall, a screen or the back of a cupboard. When the space has been decided consider the following:

- How many children are going to be allowed to work here at any one time?
- How is the area going to be kept tidy? A waste bin is an essential as there is bound to be wasted paper especially if children are going to be encouraged to cut and stick pictures or flaps in books. Perhaps the children could take it in turns to make sure everything is kept tidy and ready for the next children to use. Try not to overload the area; six well-sharpened pencils are better than a tray of assortments.
- How is the area going to be introduced to the children? They will need to be shown how to use any equipment that might be included, e.g. paper clips, clipboards. Once in use the adult should occasionally refer to the writing that takes place there, sharing pieces with other children.

Possible resources

- pens, pencils, felt tips, sharpeners, erasers, sticky tape, stapler, glue, scissors, paper clips
- paper of different types, colours and sizes, both lined and unlined; scrap paper for trying things out; card, envelopes, labels, Post-its, postcards
- blank forms, coupons, diaries, calendars
- storage items such as paper trays, pen pots, drawers, wall pockets
- subsidiary items such as stencils, rulers, guide lines, paper trimmer, typewriter, computer, book-making materials
- somewhere to display and store the children's writing.

What can children write?

Children can write for a range of purposes which can be stimulated by providing examples of writing, such as magazines, recipes, shopping lists, stories. Children can write letters. The addition of a post box from time to time can be a strong motivator for this. Suggestions of what children can write could be displayed on a poster so that the adult has instant access to ideas. This poster could include pictograms which the children could then read independently. Children will often want to copy an adult so when you write with children, perhaps a short shared story or an alternative version of Humpty Dumpty, put it in the writing area for children to use later. Sometimes the writing area can be given over to a particular focus, as commonly found in imaginative play areas. It could become a newspaper office or a card manufacturing factory.

Consider also setting the area close to the book area so that authors and favourite texts can have their influence. The writing area must be kept alive and inviting by reviewing and updating the resources and the stimuli for writing on a regular basis.

6.6 Writing in focused activities

Shared writing

A major strategy in this area is called shared writing. This is where the adult and children negotiate content and the adult models process and transcription. Shared writing is usually talked about in tandem with shared reading, using enlarged texts and you can read about this in Chapter 3. Shared reading and writing serve a number of purposes and rather than offer them here as separate examples we have prepared a sequence of activity which assumes that the adult will choose from the range of possibilities as appropriate.

Purposes

- to encourage children to work as part of a group in composing shared texts;
- to enable children to make up their own stories in collaboration with helpful others;
- to teach children that words and pictures carry meaning through the composition of their own texts;
- to introduce children to the different purposes of writing;
- to learn about the organisation of texts, that print is read from left to right and from top to bottom;
- to respond to a variety of texts including stories, songs, nursery rhymes and poems.

Organisation

You will need an easel or big book stand so that your writing is clearly visible to the children. You will also need a variety of felt-tipped pens and several large sheets of paper attached to the easel, usually by a large paper clip or similar device. Seat yourself on one side of the easel so that you are able to write on the sheets of paper without obscuring the children's view. The children will be seated at your feet. If you do not have an easel you can work on sheets of paper on the floor but you need to group children beside you so that they can see your writing in the correct orientation.

Activity

This will depend on the chosen learning intention or focus. Using the purposes above, we will offer alternatives. For all activities explain to the children what kind of writing you will be doing, who the writing is for and what the writing is to achieve.

1. The children and adult work together to write an innovation on a text. Here, a known text such as a favourite story or rhyme is used as a basis for an alternative version. 'Where's Spot?' can become 'Where's teacher?' The rhythm and pattern of the language remains intact but a few of the words are changed. Here is an innovation on Humpty Dumpty:

Edward Roberts sat on a wall,
Edward Roberts had a great fall,
All the mothers and all the children,
Couldn't make him better again.

Figure 6.8 Shared writing

2. The children and adult brainstorm the characters and plot for a story using the framework of a favourite fairy story, e.g. Jack and the Beanstalk. It can help to make a pictorial story plan with the children first. Following this the adult and children use the plan to create the text and the adult scribes. The children then decide who is going to do the illustrations for the book, which, when complete, will join the other books in the book area. Remember to include the names of the authors and illustrators.

3. Using photographs or drawings relating to a common theme, e.g. birthdays, the adult arranges them on an easel and asks the children to say what is happening. There would be negotiation over the words which could accompany them to make them into an information text for people who did not know what birthdays were, perhaps a boy from another planet.

4. Over a period of time the adult and children would compose texts which were designed for different purposes. Sometimes this would be messages of congratulations, best wishes, condolences, etc. for putting inside a card. At other times it could be a poster to show how to care for an animal or the environment. It is important that shared writing is not only seen as a strategy for story writing, and that all texts are not extended texts but also captions, etc.

5. At the final stage or publication of any of the above, the adult models explicitly the transcriptional process. Previously, s/he would have been crossing out, making changes to the order of the text, etc. The focus here would be on talking to the children about the print, how the writing is placed on the page, how the letters are formed, how punctuation is used, etc. Remember to ask as well as tell, 'Where shall I start the writing?' 'Who can find the letter 'a' in the room?' 'Who knows what this (?) is?'

6. A written response to a story might include a new ending, the introduction of a new

character, a change in the plot, a change to the setting in either time or place, another point of view, e.g. how the wolf feels. Other responses might include writing a letter to an author, making a recommendation to others to read it, making a list of similar stories which might be enjoyed.

The process

During the shared writing session try to remember that you are modelling a range of writing skills. Try to keep your original intention as a focus and do not try to teach too much in any given session. Also remember that shared writing is about negotiation and joint decision-making, so make the session as interactive as possible, inviting children to come up and write, cross out or draw from time to time.

The use of big books and shared reading is an attempt to reproduce for a group the intimacy and the interactiveness of the adult, the child and the text as it is experienced on a one-to-one basis at bedtime. Shared writing is an opportunity to reproduce the atmosphere which might be experienced as an adult helps a child to write to Grandma or make their own shopping list; it should be warm, supportive and enabling.

6.7 Writing in the environment

The resources needed for writing have already been listed. Accessibility is vital if these resources are to serve the wider writing community. This section is about the writing community, the company of writers who will stimulate and support children in their development as writers. We want to call all the people who make up this company authors, from the parent helper who writes her shopping list with the children to the significant authors referred to in Chapter 3. The writing environment should have examples of authors' work as resources and on display. The following are ways of bringing authors and their writing to children.

Displaying writing

The display areas should include a wide variety of text types, both printed and hand-written. The variety of written forms might be found in/on:

- an area where postcards and letters from friends can be collected. A pinboard or a washing line and pegs could be useful here;
- a message board where adults and children can display messages to each other;
- a story wall. Children can draw pictures from favourite stories or rhymes and these can be displayed in sequence with the text running underneath. If this is placed low down then it can be used for a shared reading activity;
- posters relating to topical issues, e.g. 'ten good reasons for going swimming'; 'our favourite nursery rhymes';
- advertisements from magazines and packaging. I remember the expressions on the faces of the four-year-olds who discovered that they could read the names from a large number of cereal packets;
- signs and labels. Make these functional; remember that one of the first things young children must learn is what writing can do. A label which says, 'now wash your hands' has much more potential for discussion and demonstration of the functions of print than a label which simply says 'pencils'. Labels which name an object which is clearly visible are superfluous; make labels meaningful as they are in the environment outside of the setting;

- a wide range of texts. These can be displayed alongside items of interest, near the pets, as part of the imaginary play area. A doctor's surgery would contain a selection of magazines and leaflets.

All of the above should be used in discussion with the children about writing; all have one or more authors behind them and part of the discussion should be about authorship. On occasions the children should meet authors so they can talk to them about their writing. In addition to the lessons children learn from other authors they learn a great deal about writing when they themselves become authors.

Making books

Identifying the audience before writing focuses the purposes and influences the outcome. Children can make books for other children, grandparents, parents, teachers and friends.

Figures 6.9 and 6.10 give some ideas for making books, some of which the children can do themselves and some of which need adult assistance.

In order for the children to become literate we need to surround them with literary events, help them to make sense of them and then support them in the creation of their own.

6.8 Assessing, recording and reporting writing

Rather than repeat here something which has been said in previous chapters about planning and assessment we want to concentrate in this chapter on analysis and response. Planning for writing involves the same principles and processes as planning for talk; they relate to your learning intentions for the children and the strategies you use to fulfil these. Can we just remind you here that intentions regarding writing will be grounded in efforts to ease the task of transcription so that children can compose at length, while encouraging independence and exploration. The checklist in Chapter 1, offered as a way of reviewing the Language and Literacy Curriculum, will serve here also as a reminder that plans need to reflect the range of variety of experiences with literacy that children need.

Assessment in general is about knowing enough about the child's experiences and understandings to make decisions which are appropriate for that child and which will take that child forward in his/her learning. We have already discussed the value of sampling children's learning through observation and collecting of drawings and photographs, etc., and what was said applies equally to assessing writing. Our focus here is on analysing and responding to children's writing.

Analysis of children's writing

'Those who make the effort ... to understand what the child is trying to say in his written expression .... will find a rich commentary on each child's earliest learning about print encapsulated in his accumulated attempts to write' (Clay 1975, p.16). To assess children's knowledge, skills, and understandings of writing it is necessary to know the individual child's progress to date. The adult in the early years setting will be selecting and keeping samples of children's drawings and writings and these should be arranged chronologically so that aspects of progress can be identified. It also helps if some of the samples are accompanied by a note explaining the context. Then the adult must work hard at converting the evidence into information which enables

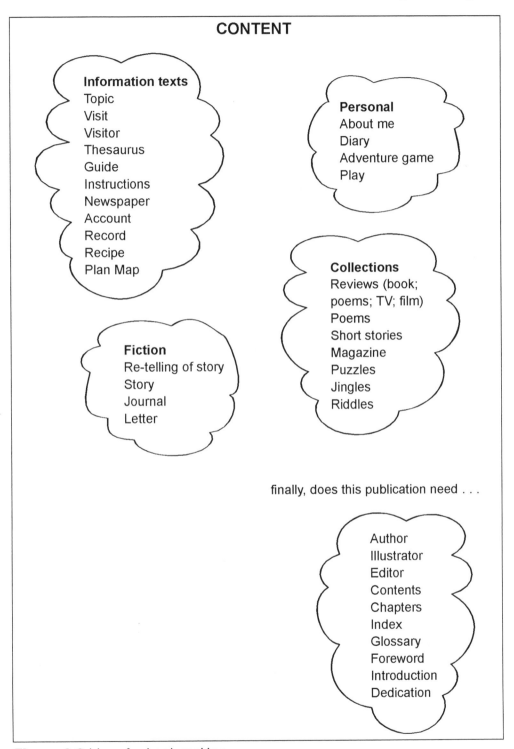

CONTENT

Information texts
Topic
Visit
Visitor
Thesaurus
Guide
Instructions
Newspaper
Account
Record
Recipe
Plan Map

Personal
About me
Diary
Adventure game
Play

Fiction
Re-telling of story
Story
Journal
Letter

Collections
Reviews (book;
poems; TV; film)
Poems
Short stories
Magazine
Puzzles
Jingles
Riddles

finally, does this publication need . . .

Author
Illustrator
Editor
Contents
Chapters
Index
Glossary
Foreword
Introduction
Dedication

Figure 6.9 Ideas for book-making

CONSTRUCTION

Folders

Folders are useful for storing drafts or for presentation.

They are useful for maps/samples for topic/notes, etc.

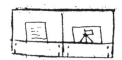

Simple books

A piece of card folded in half makes a quick simple book for the youngest children (used birthday cards are ideal).

Flip-over books

Practical hints:

1 Ring reinforcers recommended
2 Strong cord
3 Cord long enough to enable the papers to flip over easily
4 Card for cover

Zig-Zag books

Thin/thick card folded or joined together by book-binding tape, glue or sticky tape

NB: Many books can be made attractive by using: flaps, pop-ups, moving parts, etc.

Figure 6.10 Constructing a book

him/her to make judgements about the child's understanding and development so far. This information then becomes the basis for decisions about the kind of learning experiences which would benefit the child in the future. So, what are we looking for? We are looking for evidence that the child is developing both in his/her concepts of authorship and in transcription.

The collection may contain about six samples over a period of as many months. We cannot set a rule such as one per month because children's learning does not progress as methodically as that; remember that it helps if the samples were saved because they showed something significant about a child's growth. Significance will be informed by the adult's current state of knowledge about the child and about language. Initially, it helps to save anything which made you say, 'That's interesting', 'I didn't know he could do that', or 'Fancy that!' In other words, start with instinct and the trust that what is significant will change as your own knowledge changes.

Perhaps the best way to introduce you to the analytical process is to show you, so can you imagine that we are sitting side by side and on the table in front of us are these three samples of writing? Forgive the liberty we take in imaging what you might say.

Me: What is your first response?

You: I would like to know how old s/he was and what s/he was doing?
(Do you see how important context is? It's almost natural to want to know these things.)

Me: Well, it's a boy, his name is Mark and he is four years old, nearly five. I wasn't there when he wrote these, but his teacher said that he chose to write them – just took himself off to the writing table and wrote them. Unfortunately we don't know why he wrote them and that would have been a very useful piece of information, wouldn't it?

You: Well yes, how are we to tell if the form of his writing was appropriate for the purpose and the audience? Do we know if he can write in different forms, say lists of instructions?

Me: No. I guess that says something about the sample? It would have helped if we had a note saying what he was doing the writing for or if we had a more selective range of samples. He clearly knows the difference between drawing and writing, but they are a bit samey, aren't they?

You: Yes, the sentences are a bit repetitive. Do you think this is an example of Clay's inventory principle, or does he need to be more adventurous? Perhaps he doesn't know how to write in different ways.

Me: I agree. Although I don't think we can make assumptions about what he doesn't know, do you? Its rather that we don't have evidence which shows that.

You: He knows about directionality. He knows about capital and lower case letters but he doesn't know how to use them ... oops, sorry ... we don't have evidence that he knows how to use them.

Me: Yes, although he does begin each sentence with a capital 'T' followed by lower case letters.

You: The teacher probably knows the answer to this one, she will have seen lots of his writing.

Me: And maybe talked about capital letters, etc. What can we say about spelling and handwriting?

You: I love his attempt at spelling 'squashing'. And his picture with the lines showing he is jumping up and down – great.

Me: Yes, I love that picture, I also love the little caterpillar at the bottom of the page about him turning into a turtle. Interesting that he didn't use the 'ing' ending in 'turning', he has it in 'sqosing'. Do you think we can say anything about auditory and visual skills?

You: Oh, yes, I think he can hear sounds in words otherwise how did he invent shark, eating, and turtle? He also has a written sight vocabulary for words like 'is', and 'me'.

Me: So, we are beginning to get an insight into Mark's knowledge about writing, aren't we? Has this been helpful to you?

Figure 6.11 Three examples of writing

You: It's been interesting, can you give me some helpful hints so that when I do this on my own I don't forget something important?

Me: Yes. Here is a list of the kinds of things you could focus on:
- purposes and audiences for writing
- variations of text-type, or genre
- relationship between writing and pictures
- principles of page-arrangement – direction and spacing
- how signs (or letters) combine to make meanings
- different forms of script – cursive, print, upper and lower case (LINC 1992, p. 32).

Remember, that when you do this for real you will know the child and will have much more information in your head than we had here. Think how much more we could have discovered if Mark's teacher had also been sitting with us, and think how much more again if Mark had been sitting with us! Once you have taken the time to give children's writing intelligent consideration, think what sharing it with the child can do. Reflecting on their work with them and highlighting their achievements can have a very positive effect on both their self-esteem and their attitudes towards themselves as writers.

Responding to children's writing

How we see ourselves as writers is affected by the responses we receive from others to our writing. The adult working in the early years setting will need to give careful consideration to the responses made to the child's writing. Before we discuss ways of responding we should introduce you to the work of the National Writing Project (Czerniewska 1989a, b). In ways similar to the National Oracy Project (Baddeley 1992), teachers and advisory teachers worked together in their classrooms exploring ways of turning theory into practice. We have extracted the following principles which emerged from the many discussions with teachers about response.

Response should encourage

We want children to write a lot and through their experiences with writing to see writing as enjoyable, as a powerful way of communicating; to see themselves as writers. From the very beginning we want them to learn about writing and behave like writers; to be able to persist when writing is difficult and challenges; to take risks and be willing to revise and change their writing; to know about writing, in all its functions and forms.

Response can come from a variety of sources. Writers need readers. Accepting that we want children to behave as writers we need to provide them with a variety of readers. Children can write for

- themselves, e.g. diaries, reminders
- their friends, e.g. letters, stories
- their parents, e.g. cards, messages
- people they don't know personally, e.g. newspapers, adverts,

and extending their writing into their role play can give them further audiences but you may need to enlist the help of a willing adult who will reply in character.

Response may suggest how the writing may be improved by the writer. 'All response implies some sort of assessment. If that assessment is available during the writing as well as at the end, new perceptions can be incorporated into the developing piece' (Czerniewska 1989b, p. 7).

In Chapter 1 we gave you a prompt sheet for recording children's development in oracy and adapted from the work of Richmond and Savva (1990). From that same source here are the prompts offered for recording children's progress in writing. Any of these could become topics for discussion with the child provided they are used appropriately, sensitively and positively. To what extent do you believe the child is able to:

- compose meaningful texts (even though control of conventions may be at an early stage)?
- use talk to compose at greater length than s/he can write down?
- make use of the supports which the teacher provides (e.g. as a scribe, print in the environment, model texts)?
- be willing to plan, review and change their compositions where appropriate?
- play write?
- confidently write his/her name?
- write in a range of forms (e.g. letters, stories)?
- write with confidence for a variety of purposes and audiences?
- collaborate with others while writing?
- share finished writing with others?
- use a mixture of invented writing, letter-like shapes, letters and drawings?
- use the appropriate orientation of writing (e.g. left to right in English)?
- identify and order the letters of the alphabet?
- show a sense of words as units of writing, with spaces between them?
- make use of capital letters, full stops and question marks with some sense of their purpose?

7: The Role of the Adult

7.1 Defining terms

This chapter has been written with the intention of expanding on the support material, 'Parents and Partners', included in the Desirable Outcomes. It may be helpful to read page 7 of the document in conjunction with this chapter. SCAA (1996) says that in a successful partnership, 'There is recognition of the expertise of parents and other adults in the family, and this expertise is used to support the learning opportunities provided within the setting' (p. 7).

The nature of this chapter means that it is necessary to clearly define the adult in the early years setting and the adult at home. For this reason the terms 'teachers' and 'parents' will be used, although it is recognised that other adults may fulfil the roles described.

As we have seen in Chapter 1 and throughout this book, the adult is a major influence on a child's language development. Since language is a social construct the premise here is that interaction with interested and helpful adults will enhance that development.

7.2 What parents do

Recognition of the expertise of parents

Parents know their children very well and this knowledge can provide the teacher with valuable information which will enhance his/her teaching of the individual child. But before we consider the individual relationships we should look for ways of generalising the parents' expertise and using this for the benefit of all the children we work with. We can do this by identifying the conditions in which parents teach their children to talk and identifying those elements which can be useful in the early years setting.

We would ask you to begin this process of identification by thinking of your own experiences as a child. Take a few moments now to reflect on what you learnt, at home, before you went to school. Perhaps you said to count, to feed yourself, to know your colours. These are the typical replies we receive from our students. Did you include talking? Very often this is an afterthought and this might be because we think of talking in much the same way as walking, it appears to be the natural thing to do. As a young mother I wanted my children to be happy, healthy, considerate, confident, well-behaved, etc. I suppose, if I'd been asked, I would certainly have said that I wanted my children to learn, but this was rarely at the forefront of my thinking. Learning at home was very much a matter of everyday living, and I had every expectation that they would talk when they were ready. Indeed, the majority of parents expect that their children will be able to talk. As we work through this and the other conditions for talk, reflect on your own experiences and see if you can relate them to what we say.

Expectation

Expectation is key in this early, natural setting where children learn so much. Parents expect their children to join in with the talk and give them lots of positive encouragement to do so. Think of all the talk which goes on around the child, talk which the child can attend to or not as s/he wishes. Most parents have, at one time or another, had cause to exclaim, 'Now where on earth did s/he pick that up!'

One day, when my son was a baby, we were walking back from the shops. It was my habit to give him a toy to play with, to keep him amused in his pram. Suddenly I noticed that his little car was missing and was about to retrace my steps looking for it. I said, 'Where's your car?' and he dived under the blanket and retrieved it! He spent the rest of the journey home repeating this performance as I kept hiding the car and repeating the question. On reflection this seems a silly thing to do but, you see, I was amazed because he was not yet talking and yet he clearly understood what I was saying. He was actively picking up language and I knew he would soon be chatting away himself.

Using talk to make meaning

By this we mean that children are surrounded by language being used in acts of meaningful communication. At the swimming pool one day I saw a very young baby and her mother in the waiting area which overlooks the pool. Clearly it was time for the older sibling to come out of the water and get dressed. The baby, only just able to stand, was banging on the glass partition and shouting in completely incomprehensible babble, but with conviction. 'That's right,' said her mother, 'You tell him ... time to get out!' At which the baby continued vociferously to urge her brother to hurry up. The mother interpreted her baby's speech, giving it meaning, making it an act of meaningful and purposeful communication. This anecdote demonstrates how eagerly adults invite babies into the talking world.

Talking in shared contexts

By this we mean that the conversations children have occur in an environment full of non-linguistic cues which support interpretation. Consider the father asking the child, 'Do you want a drink?' This usually takes place close to a fridge or squash bottle and dad often has a cup in his hand. His features will indicate that a question is being asked. Should the child initiate the conversation, perhaps by the use of the single word 'drink', the father is able to determine, from the context, whether the child wants a drink, has spilt a drink, is offering a drink. These interactive, meaningful conversations take place embedded in the current situation which in itself gives powerful messages.

Acceptance and positive reinforcement

When a father deduces that his child would like a drink his response reinforces this and he says something like, 'Oh, you'd like a drink, would you? Milk or juice?', accompanied by similar paralinguistic support as before. The entire interaction is one of meaningful communication where the child is rewarded (with a drink) even though there is a wide linguistic gap between his utterance and adult competence. The child is accepted as a learner.

Models

By this we mean that more experienced users of language will be giving children examples of speech used to question, to explain, to joke, to empathise, to plan, to argue, etc. In a range of interactions such as the above, children are introduced to many models of speech being used in a variety of ways, and receive lots of opportunities to practise their emerging skills.

The key conditions, then, which support children when they are learning to talk are that there is an expectation that they will succeed; they hear people talking in meaningful ways; their talk is embedded in shared and purposeful contexts; they get lots of models of talk and invitations to join in, and their early attempts are received positively, responded to, and encouraged.

Are you able to make sense of the above conditions by transferring them to your own experiences? Can you translate them into a set of principles aimed at supporting the learning opportunities provided in the early years setting? Of course there are major differences between what happens in the home and what happens in the nursery. The teacher will have explicit objectives relating to language development, and will have to be able to communicate what they are and how they are going to work towards them. The setting you work in will have language policies regarding this and you should refer to these.

Parents' expertise is used to support the learning opportunities provided within the setting. As well as aims and objectives, policies usually contain principles which guide the activities of the setting: perhaps they use phrases similar to these. We intend to provide children with:

- an environment that has high expectations that they will achieve;
- opportunities to practise speaking and listening, reading and writing, by surrounding them with meaningful, purposeful, whole language;
- many models of speaking and listening, reading and writing which are heavily embedded in meaningful, functional contexts;
- feedback which accepts and encourages children as learners and which responds to the messages they convey.

Can you see the link between these policy statements and the conditions highlighted above? When the above principles underpin practice, then we, the teachers, will have begun to use the expertise of the parents.

Parental involvement in the setting

We can further use parents' expertise by inviting them to join us in the setting and work directly with the children. The preschool setting, while incorporating the best of the home environment, presents the child with an extension to his/her social world and a variety of new linguistic encounters which s/he has to interpret. Your role, as the child's teacher, is to enable the child to take full part in the life of the nursery and to organise the environment so that it enhances and extends the child's linguistic capabilities.

What do teachers do to enhance children's linguistic development, what is their role?

1. *They organise the room so that children get the opportunity to talk, read, write in a variety of different contexts with a variety of different speakers/listeners.*

The activity for the parent should develop from your plans for the children's learning. You should communicate your expectations to the parent, and the children will enjoy having another adult to talk and play with. You may need to remind the parent that your aim is for the children to be active and independent. Some parents view helping as doing things *for* the children rather than *with* them, and many will be surprised at how much the children do for themselves.

Your resources should be arranged to maximise the opportunity for children to work independently. Parents also appreciate easy access to materials; make sure all resources the parents need are available and in good condition. If the parents are working directly with the children check that they are happy to sit at low tables, on the floor, etc. If they are working to support you, for example by preparing dressing up clothes or making books, then consider providing them with adult furniture and appropriate work space.

In our experience parents like to attend a complete session, arriving and leaving with their own child. This means you have to think about their role at times when you may be telling a story or getting children ready to go home. Do not assume that parents will instinctively know what to do. In the early stages you will need to be explicit and confident enough to direct another adult. As you get to know each other you will find many parents sensitive to the demands of your role and able to play a very positive part in supporting your work.

2. *They find real purposes or contexts in which children's language can be developed and extended in meaningful ways.*

Parents are invaluable in this respect. Spend time finding out what events/occasions are imminent and incorporate them in your plans. Children love to make cards and design invitations for an aunt's wedding, for example. The local community is another opportunity to find real contexts for oracy and literacy learning.

Make some trips that have a literacy emphasis. For example, a visit to a local shop could involve a joint letter to the shopkeeper asking permission, a list of questions for the children to ask the shopkeeper during interview, a shopping list of items to be bought, maps showing the journey/imaginary journeys, collecting packaging for display, thank you letters for posting to the shopkeeper and notification to the local newspaper. Use your local environment, your community, your children's experiences and most of all ... your and the children's imaginations!

3. *They take part in the task, actively listening to parents' comments and observations, and helping them to work and play together, explore language (by introducing new varieties and forms) and reflect on what they have done and said.*

You and the staff will be important models for the parents. They will watch your behaviour with the children and may imitate the way you talk with children and the way you encourage children to ask questions, etc. Being observed by another adult can feel uncomfortable and many experienced teachers admit to feeling embarassed or tense in such a situation. It helps to remember that the parents are only trying to learn from you, so try to take time to explain why you act the way you do. I remember one occasion when I was in my first year of teaching. A parent came into my reception class to help with clay; I settled her and six children to the task and left to work with another group of children. When I returned later I found the children had all left and the parent was engrossed in squeezing and moulding a lump of clay. She appeared oblivious to what was going on around her and so I left her. I don't know what made me decide to do this but later she confided that she had never used clay before and that she had thoroughly enjoyed it. It transpired that she was going through a very difficult time at home and had found the experience therapeutic and relaxing.

I use this story to illustrate that activity does not always go according to plan. A common occurrence is that a parent arrives unexpectedly and offers to help. You could, quite reasonably, politely ask if they can come back another time as you are not prepared for them. On the other hand, and this is a personal view, you could be prepared for this possibility and have a set of impromptu tasks for the parent:

- Write your shopping list. Tell the children what you are doing and why.
- Browse in the book area and talk about the books with any interested children.
- Parallel play. Sit at the dough table and do as the children are doing. Talk about how it feels, what they can do with it, what it is made of, etc.
- Empty your bag/pocket (not valuables!) and share paper items, e.g. driving licence, till receipt, library ticket. Ask children what they think they are, what are they for, who wrote them, why?
- Play a board game. (It helps if the game includes a 'Parents' prompts' telling parents how to get the best from it for the children, etc.).
- Write a letter to a friend/pet/toy. Encourage children to do the same.
- Read your newspaper/book to yourself. Encourage children to ask you questions about what you are doing.

4. *They provide resources and information that will interest and enable children.*

In the section dealing with research you will learn that one of the major influences on the quality of talk in the early years setting depends on shared experiences. By encouraging children to bring resources from home you are doing two things. Firstly you are enabling the children to bring to the setting experiences from the home. Secondly you are demonstrating that you value their home life. You need the kind of information children and parents bring to the setting in order to engage fully in meaningful conversation with the children. However, you should be aware of your role concerning the use of home resources. You must first be sure that they are appropriate for the purpose and the children. They must be safe (consider the lead content of old toys, for example).

You must also make sure that parents are willing for children to handle/play with their property. In the best environment accidents can happen and you should be clear what the possible consequences might be should damage occur. These things established, you will find parents a rich source of material which will interest and engage young children.

We urge you to consult the policies and to talk to other staff members before you embark on any form of parental involvement. This is an area where whole school commitment is vital and these are the sort of issues you need to consider:

- Are you going to invite all parents into the teaching areas? If not, what are your criteria for inclusion/exclusion, and how are you going to apply these fairly and consistently?
- Are you going to welcome siblings? If not, you will exclude many parents who do not have ready access to child care for younger brothers and sisters.
- Are you going to have an open policy (where parents can come and help at random moments) or are you going to set aside predetermined times for such help?
- Are you going to talk to parents initially about things such as confidentiality, your expectations, their expectations, how to work with a group of children?
- Are you going to be able to find time to listen to parents' views on how it went?

Remember that you are responsible for what happens in your setting and you must be able to articulate the aims and objectives which have led to any decisions you make regarding parental involvement. As in all areas of the curriculum, parental involvement requires a high degree of planning and preparation.

It is important to recognise that some parents feel a loss of expertise when their child enters a more formal educational setting. They can feel uneasy in an early years setting, and for many this may be the first time since they themselves were at school. As you set up your environment to welcome parents think always of ways you can make them feel comfortable and truly welcome.

Partnership with parents

Although they may feel less confident in the above setting they are fully confident in their knowledge of their own child and this brings us to another area of expertise which needs to be recognised. Parents are experts when it comes to knowing their own child. When we talk about using this individual expertise in the early years setting we are usually talking about a partnership with parents, a partnership which focuses on the individual child.

What do we mean by partnership? How is it possible to attain partnership which could suggest equal involvement/responsibility? Of course, the relationship will not be equal since, as we have seen, parents and teachers have different roles. As stated earlier, one fundamental difference is that the professional has carefully considered goals for children's development. S/he also has a range of strategies for attaining these goals which are underpinned by a knowledge and understanding of education and children as learners. The aims and objectives are open for inspection by interested parties which include parents and the local community. The teacher has to be able to communicate and justify the practice in nursery, and this includes the role of parents. We urge you to consult the policies and to talk to other staff members before you embark on any form of parental involvement. Many good intentions have faltered due to insufficient sensitivity and poor communication.

A sensible interpretation of the concept of partnership here is that the members of the partnership recognise and value the strengths that each brings and are willing to actively work together to promote the child's learning in an atmosphere that is sensitive and supportive. Discussion on how such a partnership might work will be found in a later section, in the meantime the concept of partnership is a complex one and should not be encouraged without careful consideration of the issues above. However, it has long been accepted by early years practitioners that a working partnership is both sensible and worthwhile. Sensible because parents and teachers share concern for the child's well-being and healthy development and because they are both key influences in the child's learning. Worthwhile because teachers recognise that their aims are more achievable when they are shared and understood by parents.

7.3 What the research says

Further argument for parental involvement in childrens' learning comes from research. Dombey wrote 'the vast battery of studies of child language carried out in the intervening 25 years has shown us that home is where the most powerful language learning takes place' (in Lightfoot and Martin 1988, p. 71).

Does this surprise you at all? What are your perceptions of the linguistic abilities of the young children you know?

Language learning in the home and nursery

Hughes (in Wray and Medwell 1994, p. 8) found that teachers of young children often conform to the deficit model of language, feeling that children come to school with speech that is limited and under-developed. Some of the teachers Hughes interviewed suggested that a possible cause of this could be found in the home environment. 'A large degree of concern was expressed about the amount and type of communication which took place at home.'

He also noted that although teachers often knew that research contradicted this they were not necessarily convinced. So, in the South West of England the University of Exeter and a local LEA undertook an Early Years Language Project to examine these perceptions. The teachers involved were surprised to find that their perceptions were not confirmed by the observations and recordings of the children's conversations at home. The children carried out complex and competent conversations at home and were supported by parents who were concerned and interested.

It seems that we are more likely to change our minds when we see something for ourselves. One project which enhanced teachers' seeing was the National Oracy Project (Baddeley 1992) which operated from September 1987 to 1993 initially in 35 local education authorities and had as one of its aims 'to enhance teachers' skills and practice'. Wells (in Norman 1992, p. 305) celebrated the achievements of the teachers involved in the National Oracy Project and said that

> Teacher research, conducted in the context of professional development, arises out of the professional concerns of individual teachers and has as its purpose to improve their practice. It is also concerned with the development of theory, but primarily with the personal theory of the teacher, as this is enriched and extended through the interplay of observation, action and reflection that occurs in the prosecution of his or her problem-based inquiry.

We urge you to develop your skills of observation and to reflect on what you see, with a view to pursing your own lines of enquiry and research. The accounts generated by the National Oracy Project include many examples of teachers raising their own questions and generating their own hypotheses and theories which they then test out against current thinking. Through these accessible stories you will be introduced to wider reading and research.

Whichever route you take to your own professional development, through personal or received hypotheses, there are two major studies which have been very influential and which you should know about. The first is the work of the aforementioned Gordon Wells (1987) and the Bristol Language Development Research Programme. This was a large-scale project where more than 100 British children wore small microphones which recorded their conversations randomly throughout the day over an extended period of time. The children's ages ranged from 15 months to 5.5 years and the resulting recordings produced a large amount of data which has subsequently been analysed.

Wells (1987) states that

all but a very small minority of children reach the age of schooling with a vocabulary of several thousand words, control of the basic grammar of the language of their community, and an ability to deploy these resources in conversations arising from the many and varied situations that occur in their everyday lives (p. 16).

A similar conclusion was reached by Tizard and Hughes (1984) who made comparisons between the language of young girls at home and at school and found that children's talk with adults was richer at home than at school.

This research made many early years practitioners, including myself, think again about the quality of talk in the nursery. We considered various explanations for the disparity in the quality of talk at home and at nursery. Was it possible that the linguistic repertoire of the nursery contained elements which were unfamiliar to the children? Who was doing the most talking, the children or us? Might all this lead to children avoiding engagement in conversation which lacks meaning or confuses? What did children make of phrases which are peculiar to school? 'Are you a packed lunch?' 'Put up your hands, red table', etc. We had to seriously re-think our perceptions regarding what we were achieving in terms of the children's language development. Above all we had to face our own preconceptions about what the children were able to do before they came to nursery. We changed our minds and changed our practice to accommodate the evidence that:

- children learn to talk at home. All homes provide a rich source of linguistic and intellectual stimulation for the developing speaker;
- there may be differences between homes but there is no suggestion that the quality of talk is any less, nor that children learn to speak any more slowly or less effectively in working-class homes than in middle class homes;
- there are important differences between the nature and style of conversations in the home and at school;
- working-class children find the move from home to school more disruptive in terms of their language development than do their middle-class counterparts.

We, the staff, re-evaluated our provision and concluded that we must do more to bring other experienced language users into the nursery to provide children with more opportunities for engaging in extended talk. It was clear to us that we had much to learn from the early language opportunities provided by the home and this led to an even greater commitment to developing strong working relationships with our children's parents.

Oracy, as a curriculum focus, is in the early stages of development relative to literacy. There have been many studies on the benefits of parental involvement in the development of their children's reading and writing but most of these have concentrated on children already in formal education. Parental involvement in literacy preschool is less widely studied. However, in 1988, the Sheffield Early Literacy Development Project compared the impact of working with parents at home and in the early years setting (Weinberger *et al.* 1990).

Working with parents in the home

In order to support the individual child's learning in school it is, of course, necessary to know that child well. To support the parents it helps to know both the child and the

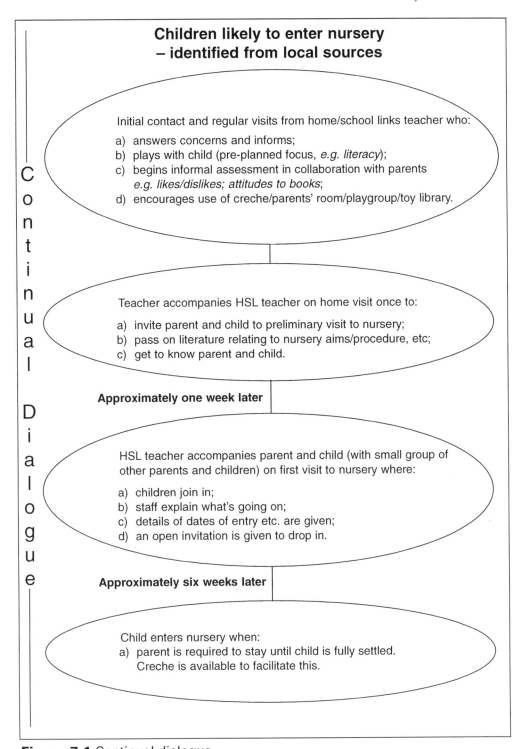

Figure 7.1 Continual dialogue

parents. Early years teachers are fortunate in this respect since they usually meet with parents when they bring and collect their children, and, as said before, it is common to welcome adults into the setting for many purposes. Some establishments, wishing to extend this on a one-to-one basis employ a teacher whose role is to introduce herself to the parents of very young babies and help them, both with the early learning of that baby and in getting to know the setting. A creche/mother–toddler group/playgroup often accompanies this facility. This is not widely adopted, however, and there are two possible reasons for this. It is very expensive to operate. As you can imagine, one teacher visiting the homes of children likely to enter the setting at a later date is very intensive and time-consuming. It is also a matter of much professional debate, where views differ greatly regarding whether or not it is valid to encroach on the personal lives of the families of the children we teach. It is clearly one thing to invite parents into our working environment and quite another to invite ourselves into their homes. This can be particularly invasive if that family are already the focus for outside intervention from other agencies.

I have experienced home visiting first hand and Figure 7.1 represents the mechanics of the system in which I operated. I found that

> parents and children tend to be more at ease in their own homes than at school. It is their territory and it is the professional who is the visitor. This helps to alter the balance of power, and makes partnership possible. Also it is easier for the home visitor to acknowledge and build on the literacy experiences the child is encountering at home (Sheffield Reading Project 1988, p. 7).

Home visiting is a sensitive area and before embarking on such a scheme you must enter the debate fully with your local authority, other agencies dealing with families and children, other early years settings, and with the parents themselves.

We would like to conclude this section as we began, by encouraging you to embark on a process of continual learning and reflection. The Sheffield Project was informed by four lines of research any one of which could provide you with a useful focus for your own research.

- Parents often respond positively to school efforts to involve them in the teaching of reading.
- Knowledge of literacy at school entry is a strong predictor of later attainment.
- Intervention in the preschool period can be effective, both in the short term and in the long term.
- Babies and young children learn about literacy through the literacy experiences in their everyday lives, together with the active engagement of someone more skilled than themselves' (Weinberger *et al.* 1990, p. 5).

Remember you have evidence in your daily working life which can make a powerful contribution to professional debate and your growing professional awareness can make a considerable contribution to your own practice.

7.4 Key concepts

Throughout this book we repeatedly make the point that language and literacy are interrelated, and this is the point at which we reaffirm this position in relation to this chapter. This is a simple process and we invite you to join us in looking over the key features of language learning at home and translating them into meaningful statements regarding reading and writing.

Expectation

We must convey to children that we expect them to be able to learn to read and write. This means more than just saying so. We must show them that we believe they can do it, by praising their efforts, by providing them with challenge and the opportunity for success, and by celebrating their achievements.

Using reading and writing to make meaning

We must emphasise to children and parents that reading and writing are systems of communication. Reading and writing mean more than getting the words right; they are also about interpreting and making sense.

Reading and writing in shared contexts

Do you remember the non-linguistic cues mentioned previously? Picture books are full of such cues. As the child reads the pictures s/he learns how it feels to take and make meaning from a page. Advertisements are similarly readable. The pictures/action continue to offer powerful support as the child begins to attend to the print. When people talk about whole language texts they mean texts which are contextualised (given meaning) by surrounding features which the child can use to support interpretation.

When you provide a context in which the child writes, e.g. a menu for the restaurant, then s/he has the task of conveying the meaning to an audience. The function of the writing must be understood by the child, so try to always offer a child a reason to write and somebody to write for.

Sharing operates on two levels: the sharing between the author and the reader and the sharing between the child and the expert reader/writer who helps the child in his/her engagement with literature.

Acceptance and positive reinforcement

We accept that it will be some time before the child displays adult competence in reading and writing. We accept their attempts while providing maximum support as they refine and develop their ability to take and make meaning through print.

Models

We provide children with models of print used in a variety of ways. We talk about them, what they are for, who they are for, etc.

The key conditions which support children when they are learning to read/write are that there is an expectation that they will succeed; they see people reading/writing in meaningful ways; their reading/writing is embedded in shared and purposeful contexts; they get many models of reading/writing and invitations to join in, and their early attempts are received positively, responded to, and encouraged.

Before we move onto the more practical section we would like to make a short summary of what we have said so far in this chapter.

We have shown you how it is possible to identify the key features of language learning at home, which has been, for the majority of children, very successful in enabling the child to become a competent talker. We suggest that you use this expertise in the early years setting by extracting the key principles which you use as a guide for practice.

We have introduced you to research evidence which emphasises the expertise of parents and compares the quality of talk in the home and in the early years setting. We have considered the issues pertaining to parental involvement in the classroom, and in working with parents in a partnership designed to promote the learning of the individual child. Our intention has been to discuss the rationale behind the philosophy of parents and teachers working together for the good of the child. We feel that we have offered you evidence and discussion which will help you to recognise the expertise of parents and acknowledge the role parents have already played so that you can assure them that they continue to have a positive role in their child's development.

7.5 Parents in play, in focused activities and in the environment

This section has a practical emphasis and uses two questions, taken from the support material offered by SCAA as a framework for the sharing of ways of working with parents (1996, p. 7).

Question 1: How can we give parents access to information about what goes on in the setting?

Provide public areas in the setting. These can be as small as a display area or as large as a parents' room. Either way the opportunity to celebrate and share the children's achievements provides you with an opportunity to communicate good practice, for example:

- photographs of children talking/reading/writing together with a caption explaining how this contributes to their oracy and literacy development;
- a book/poster of ideas for activities which parents might like to do with their children. Look in published material for ideas; often teachers' handbooks have chapters, games, etc. which parents might like to play. Try to indicate how these are helping so that parents can begin to see why you do certain things. Perhaps you can offer a library facility where parents can borrow published material which you can recommend;
- a notice board area where you can leave general messages about the curriculum: 'Next week we are having a visit from the local shopkeeper. We are particularly looking at cereal packaging. Can you talk to your child about what they see in the shops? Perhaps you could send in some empty packages?' In my nursery we had a 'graffiti' board which was a white board so that parents could reply to messages like the above.

Provide literature (in different languages where appropriate). The quality of the communication between nursery and parents is fundamental to the success of any model of parental partnership.

Communication in the printed form requires awareness of audience. Please remember that some parents may have difficulty with reading and writing, or perhaps they do not have good command of English. Keep the text clear, concise, and jargon-free without becoming patronising. We suggest that you ask one or two parents to preread a draft of any letter you are sending out widely so that you can avoid misunderstandings. Some schools have taped versions of letters for parents who cannot read, and some have letters and tapes in different languages. All of these are made available through a process which is discreet and sensitive to parents' feelings. Some examples are:

- a brochure all about the setting, with a section relating to curriculum;
- a leaflet specifically to do with language. Remember to explain what you are doing and why, in a way that is unambiguous;
- a newsletter which might contain forthcoming events, articles written by other parents, etc.

Some settings have a video showing the learning areas in the setting, with a voice-over explaining what the children are learning when they are sharing books, writing lists, playing with blocks, etc.

- Welcome visits into the setting, but always try to find a way to explain what visitors see. For example, if a teacher is observing a group of children a parent may not understand that this is part of good teaching. They may interpret this as 'doing nothing'.

Encourage parents to come:

- as helpers. To tell personal stories to children. To be interviewed by the children. To play a game with the children. This list is endless but remember to plan what the parent is to do and to communicate this to him/her. Give him/her the opportunity to choose from a selection of possibilities as s/he may not be comfortable in certain situations. Remember also that many parents have hidden talents. You may have an artist/musician/author/inventor in your midst.
- for social events. Even the most informal event such as a quiz night or a barn dance is an opportunity to communicate. When parents come into the setting they will always look around, so look around in advance and see what messages the environment is sending.
- for meetings. These can vary from more formal presentations of curriculum and policy to less formal occasions where parents might simply be invited in to browse through the book stock or engage in some of the activities which the children undertake on a regular basis. Both of these with the intention that the discussion focus on what children might be learning.

One nursery I know runs a series of workshops for parents interested in helping their children with literacy. The parents themselves made a poster for parents and visited the local library.

Communicating to parents in any of the ways above will give parents the information they need in order to make sense of what happens in the setting. However, there can be a gap between what happens in nursery and how that is translated in practice at home. When you have established confidence in parents that they have already taught their children many things and that the skills they have in so doing will support future learning; when you have open lines of effective communication between home and the setting; when you have carefully considered plans for involving parents in the nursery and when you are genuinely prepared to listen to

WHY?
Children who read at home with a caring grown up get on better in school.

WHEN?
Every day if you can manage it – 10 minutes a day will really help.

WHAT?
They need lots of praise and encouragement.

They need your special help.

They need to enjoy and look forward to reading time with you.

S/he will learn to read by reading lots of books which s/he can manage easily.

We will try to send home books that are fun.

NOTHING SUCCEEDS LIKE SUCCESS!

Figure 7.2 Reading at home

parents and value their role you have achieved a great deal which contributes to an effective partnership.

Question 2: How can we help continuity by suggesting ways parents can help at home?

General suggestions for all parents can be communicated individually or through any of the above-mentioned media.

- Talk with your child about everyday activities and things that interest him/her. Tell him/her stories and say/sing nursery rhymes/TV jingles together. Take every opportunity to talk with your child about the things you see, hear and do. Encourage your child to share opinions, to ask questions, to explain. Play with words and talk about talking, reading and writing.
- Read with your child, looking at the pictures and encouraging your child to join in when s/he wants to. Build up a set of favourite stories which your child knows well. Point out print in the environment and let him/her see you and others reading.
- Encourage your child to play with pencil and paper. Give him/her lots of different writing implements and materials to experiment with. Encourage him/her to 'write' alongside you: shopping lists, reminders, letters, postcards or instructions.

These are the basic messages to be conveyed to parents. There are numerous examples of how early years settings have taken these and publicised them in their own way by:

- adding photographs from their own settings;
- including examples of childrens' drawings and writings so that parents know what to expect (Fig 7.2);
- providing lists of books which they and their children might enjoy;
- giving examples of games to play;

What if they get stuck on a word?

- Don't make too much of it.
- Don't ask them to sound it out.
- Ask them what the word might be.
- Give them time to think and let them have a go.
- Ask if it makes sense and sounds right.
- Ask them to check by looking again at the word in the text – especially the first letter.
- If they still don't know – tell them – and ask them to read that bit again – or read it yourself.

Figure 7.3 Stuck on a word

- providing books, games, etc. on loan. Some nurseries operate a toy library;
- providing taped stories which could be recorded by parents;
- making suggestions for individual children (Fig. 7.3).

Most early years settings pay particular attention to welcoming parents on visits before the children begin attending and by encouraging them to stay with their child until the child feels settled. Because of this open attitude much of what has previously been mentioned takes place informally. Also, because of this, many settings have no formal policy for talking to parents individually. Sometimes when the setting is in a school, the practice of open nights is carried into the nursery class and operates along similar lines. With the advent of greater accountability and the emphasis on preschool assessment many establishments will be looking for models of parent interviews which ensure that all parents have the opportunity to talk with the staff about their child. Again, whichever setting you find yourself in it is recommended that you find out what policies and practice already exist. Perhaps you are in a setting which is looking to develop or modify a system to suit the parents of young children? In this case we would like to talk to you about literacy conferences in the following section.

7.6 Planning, assessment and recording

Over the course of time, following the suggestions in other chapters, you will have collected a range of evidence relating to each child's progress and learning. You may have kept a selection of observation notes, examples of children's work, and photographs which could be used to form a profile of the child's development over a period of time. These could be used as a focus of discussion between you and the child's parents.

We would like to return to *The Primary Language Record* (Barrs *et al.* 1988), a package produced for primary schools which sets out a comprehensive set of procedures for recording children's progress in oracy and literacy. It also includes detailed descriptions of ways of undertaking regular conferences with children and parents. The handbook is accessible and the chapter regarding the discussion between the parent and the teacher is particularly helpful here, despite its being designed for children of statutory school age. *The Primary Language Record* has several features which could reasonably be adopted by the early years practitioner.

1. It uses evidence of achievement as a vehicle for discussion. This means that the discussion uses examples of what the child does or says as a vehicle for assessing development and progress. This has the potential to be a powerful source of dialogue regarding what we see as progress. Simply comparing a drawing done on entry to the setting with one done several months later can be very useful strategy for assessing the success of the teaching and learning. The same applies for other samples you might keep. Of course you need the agreement of the child that a particular picture or model can be kept rather than sent home immediately, but I have found most children amenable to the idea that they have a special folder or container which is being saved so that it can be shown to their parents later.
2. It records parents' comments in collaboration with the teacher. This enables progression from one meeting to the next. This means that parents can feel genuinely included in their child's learning, and that their contributions are valued and listened to. We ought to make it clear that this is undertaken in a shared situation where comments are negotiated and views from both parties are given equal weight. The end point of one discussion can become the beginning of the next, thereby making it possible to gain a sense of continuity and forward movement rather than a summing up of the past.
3. It gives parents the opportunity to comment on the child's progress in talking, reading and writing. This means that you have access to information which can inform your future plans and response to that child. What you know about a child affects what you say to the child. *The Primary Language Record* has a useful list of topics for discussion during a conference, which they envisage lasting approximately 20 minutes.

In addition to directing you to the above as a source of useful information, we would like to add a few of our own thoughts. Remember that your formative assessments will be in direct relationship to your plans, in particular to your learning intentions for that child. When you talk to parents about their child's performance remember to put it in the context of what you wanted him/her to learn and how you went about it.

You should practise confidentiality and not record or repeat detailed discussions with parents which they would not like made public. What you record should be with the complete understanding and agreement of the parent concerning its use. You should exercise discretion at all times and be sensitive to parents' needs. Be aware that some parents may need support, for example when their first language is not English.

The context of discussion with parents should be seen as an opportunity for both parties to learn from each other and as a result make a positive contribution to the child's development.

8: Play: Making the Whole

8.1 Defining terms

The role of play in the early years is established and has permeated every topic throughout this book. Explicit references can be found in the Desirable Outcomes including, 'through art, music, dance, stories and imaginative play, they show an increasing ability to use their imagination, to listen and observe' (Creative Development) and 'approaches to teaching include recognition of ... appropriate adult intervention and of using play and talk as media for learning' (Common Features of Good Practice) and 'take part in role play with confidence' (Language and Literacy).

This chapter is about using play as a positive teaching strategy which may include the active involvement of the adult. We offer ideas for the imaginative play area and for ways of playing with words. We also offer a diagrammatic representation of the process of planning, assessment, recording and reporting.

8.2 Play in the curriculum

We do not attempt to present a rationale for play in the early years curriculum. We assume that the reader will recognise what Meadows (1992) calls the classic early childhood curriculum, describing it as one 'which provides children in settings such as playgroups and nursery schools with materials and opportunities for play and encourages them in self-chosen means-dominated activities rather than involving them in achievement-directed training'.

The work of Susan Isaacs (1929) was very influential in the movement towards free play in early years settings. She saw play as essential to a child's physical, social, emotional and cognitive development. Other researchers have recorded the value of play in a variety of ways:

- as a way of releasing excess energy (Spencer 1878)
- as a way of practising the skills needed for life (Groos 1901)
- as a re-enactment of evolution (Hall 1908)
- as a cathartic when used to express anxiety (Freud 1923)
- as a mastery of existing skills (Piaget 1951)
- as a way of solving problems (Sylva 1977).

It is becoming clear why play is so central to the early years curriculum.

Language and literacy underpin all aspects of life; we use both spoken and written language to

- communicate with each other
- explore the environment
- establish and clarify ideas
- question and maintain the normal pattern of life.

Young children are empowered as they learn to use language to achieve their own aims and meet their needs. The parallels with play become stronger as we consider the five justifications made by Cox (DES 1989, paras. 2.20–2.27) for the place of English in the curriculum.

Cox argued that children need familiarity with, confidence and expertise in language because they need it in order to succeed in adult life. As in play children rehearse elements of mature life, so in their language use they rehearse the power and effect of language on others.

Secondly, language is a means of passing on the cultural heritage of a society; Cox argued that it is the responsibility of the school 'to lead children to an appreciation of those works of literature that have been widely regarded as the finest in the language'. The work of Heath (1983) illustrates how children learn the values and practices of literacy which are specific to their own community and which do not always match those of the school. It is incumbent on teachers to know 'where children are coming from' in their understandings of language and literacy and to introduce children to other ways of using literacy which may be used in the wider world. Play is the most natural way to introduce these ideas.

Thirdly, just as play allows children to act out and explore their own feelings and attitudes, so, Cox argued, can language develop children's 'imaginative and aesthetic lives'. As children perhaps play out events in their own lives in an attempt to come to terms with them, hearing stories about similar experiences can help children to understand and not feel quite so alone.

Language is also the medium of instruction and so is essential for all children, to enable them to make the most of the opportunities that are offered them. Lastly, Cox saw language as helping children towards a 'critical analysis of the world and the cultural environment in which they live'. This ability to question and explore ideas, behaviours and attitudes is one which truly empowers and language, literacy and play can help young children to do this within a safe and controlled context.

Spend time observing children at play and you will soon be able to identify what it is the children are actually learning. The quality of play and how it affects learning has been the focus of many studies. Meadows (1992) found that 'Much of what children did when playing was pleasurable but simple, repetitive, unstructured, uninventive, brief and generally uninspiring' (p. 66). Bennett and Kell (1989) also found that much of the play they observed lacked purpose and challenge. Certainly we recognise that children need space and time to play alone and with peers, without direct adult intervention. However, what the children are doing has, in a sense, already been subject to adult intervention – the provision itself involves choices and decisions regarding what the children will play with.

Indirect intervention

By this we mean the kinds of intervention that take place distanced from the child, for example, the way the play space and equipment is organised, the variety of starting points offered and the timings of and within sessions. In general, it concerns the decisions and plans we make in order to meet the desired goals. In reading, the adult might select from a variety of texts according to the demands of the activity and the interests of the child. In writing, the adult may leave models of a particular form in the writing area so that children may have access to different ways of presenting writing. In speaking and listening the adult may create time for one child to tell his/her story to a group of children or another adult. As has already been said, the decisions we make are related to the intentions we have.

Children also have intentions. The classic curriculum described above derives in part from the belief that children can and should be autonomous in their learning, choosing from a menu of activities carefully provided to ensure all-round development. The theme of child independence and selectivity runs through the Desirable Outcomes when they say children should be able to do such things as 'demonstrate independence in selecting an activity or resources' (p. 2) and 'explore and select materials and resources' (p. 4).

So, decisions regarding resources, the allocation of time and the activities provided cannot be made in isolation from the needs and interests of the children both as a group and as individuals. Some of the plans should be made in consultation with the children. For planning to be effective it needs to reflect the objectives of the establishment and the needs of the children. The Desirable Outcomes are a framework for planning in response to individual needs, and knowledge of those needs comes from interaction with the child and his/her family.

Direct intervention

This refers to those occasions when the adult and the child work, talk and play together. Bennett and Kell (1989) emphasise the need for increased adult involvement in children's play. Hendy (1995) argues this in a specific reference to language work, when she says 'by engaging in children's story making in an active and participatory manner I have uncovered depths of understanding and complexity of ideas that are difficult to tap in the ordinary everyday activities of the best classroom'. Joining in children's play is a strategy often overlooked in the busy early years setting. Sometimes the status of play is marginalised to the extent that it becomes an opportunity for adults to do other things or for children to do when they have finished other activities which can assume more importance. This vastly undervalues the importance of play.

Taking part in children's play

When we take part in children's play we are able to:

Assess

We can learn about the children, their skills, knowledge and understandings which are revealed in the variety of contexts that play offers. Hutt (1989) found that when children were engaged in fantasy play their utterances were longer, they used more adverbs and used modal auxiliary verbs more frequently than when they were engaged in non-fantasy sessions. It is play which gives the children the opportunity to use and us the opportunity to observe this type of language use.

Model

An adult playing with children can add extra dimensions to that play. S/he can model the consequences of an action, for example, how a character talks when angry or sad; s/he can model processes of sharing and negotiation, especially when the adult role in the play has equal status and relevance to that of the child.

Sustain

When the play becomes repetitive or uninspiring the adult can change the direction, often picking up on the children's own ideas, which might have been unrecognised and therefore not followed through.

Extend

The adult can introduce resources into the play, for example, bringing out a map or drawing road signs if the children are going on an imaginary trip. The play can also be enriched by the introduction of new concepts.

Collaborate

The adult and the child can work together, each contributing ideas and responding to the ideas of the other. The child can assume the expert role and the adult can question and seek explanation. Both can take part in the problem-identifying and problem-solving process.

Support and respond

The adult can encourage, praise and enable the children to fulfill their own expectations. Children who are shy or reticent can be helped to take part. When children reach a barrier to their continued play the adult can often help the child to overcome this and enable play to continue.

Direct intervention in children's play can present similar opportunities for furthering learning to intervention in other more focused activities. It is one of many teaching strategies but there are two cautions which must be sounded.

The first is the concept of ownership. Children initiate play for a variety of reasons and the adult needs to consider carefully whether the changes that will inevitably occur when s/he enters the play will be at the expense of other possibly more valid outcomes. S/he also needs to be aware that, because of the established roles, children will readily give control to the adult. The sensitive adult will avoid taking over and will use their professional judgement in deciding when it is appropriate to enter and leave the play situation.

The second is to do with those roles previously mentioned. The adult will have assumed a role of authority and the children may, at first, find it difficult to adapt to the change from authority to partner in play. One way to introduce children to the idea that the adult has these different roles is to begin with simple role play. Story is an excellent vehicle for this. Try taking on the role of a character from a story and asking the children to ask you questions. When we first do this with young children they sometimes look disconcerted, but when we explain that we are playing and are not really that character they soon respond with enthusiasm. You need a certain amount of confidence to join in child's play. Do not confuse this with being childlike – we are definitely not advocating that you take on the persona of a four-year-old. Children take play seriously and if the adult joins in then s/he should do so with commitment to the role. Together adult and child create alternative happenings; they do not work to a script or act in the theatrical sense of the word.

Throughout this book there have been references to role play and the imaginative play area. The definition of role play which has guided our thinking is that it is the exploration of situations, where children can take on other roles and experiences which might help them learn about themselves and others.

Why role play?

- It helps children learn about relationships and develop social skills.
- The language used can be extended and developed in the context of a stimulated 'real' experience.

- Children can meet challenges and uncertainties, taking part in problem solving-processes.
- It can extend children's thinking by introducing new concepts and perspectives.
- The opportunities it provides for self-expression can enhance self-image and confidence.
- It can be cathartic, children can work through possible dilemmas associated with real experience in a non-threatening environment.

The development of language can be enhanced when an adult enters the play. S/he has the advantage of being able to introduce new vocabulary and ways of using words. Sometimes the play will actually be with words; playing with language can be seen as having similar properties to playing with paints or with construction toys. Through play the child explores the 'object', in this case words, and discovers how they can be used. Hutt (1989) suggests that play could be subdivided into two imaginary questions which the child is trying to answer. The first is 'What does this do?' (exploration) and the second is 'What can I do with this?' (play). Children need the opportunity to explore spoken and written language to see what it does and then to take control of it in order to discover what they can do with it. They need to play with language.

Parents and adults in the early years setting who encourage children to play with language, using jingles, rhymes, jokes, nonsense words and, in particular, nursery rhymes, are making it possible for the child to pay attention to the sounds of the words, the rhythms of the language, the meanings, the large and small detail and potential of language. The role of the adult here is to provide children with the context for language development, the environment and the opportunities, and then to play, enjoy and talk with children about language.

8.3 Playing with language in focused activities

This section invites you to capitalise on children's willingness to play with words. You have only to eavesdrop on the playground games of primary aged children to experience their ability to invent and pass on a rich tradition of rhymes and games. Think of the games you played as a child; perhaps you sang skipping songs:

All in together girls,
Never mind the weather girls,
O-U-T spells Out!

or clapping songs:

Oranges and lemons say the bells of St. Clement's.
I owe you five farthings say the bells of St. Martin's.

ball songs:

Betty Grable is a star S-T-A-R

or dips:

Ip, dip, sky blue, who's it? Not you.
O – U – T spells Out!'

These come from our memories and belie our age. You will have a different repertoire and so will the children you know. This section is about building a wide repertoire of language games that can be played at any time, with few resources. If you are a beginner in this area try the well-known favourite 'Ring-o-roses' and seek out texts which contain similar games.

Language games

Here are some language games which we have played and which you might find useful:

Story round
Sit in a circle and retell a well-known story or rhyme, each child contributing the next few words or sentences.

Tongue twisters
Simple tongue twisters can be fun. Try 'Red lorry, yellow lorry' and see what happens.

Name rhymes
Make up rhymes for children's names, e.g. 'Robert, Robert likes strawberry yogurt.'

Clapping rhythm
Clap to any song but also clap the rhythm of children's names. Try clapping the rhythm of well-known nursery rhymes and see if the children can recognise them.

Not now, Bernard
One child is chosen to be Bernard's mum. S/he stands, back to the group, and listens while one child says simply 'Hello mum' in his/her own voice. Mum has to guess who said it and reply 'Not now —'. On the correct guess the child assumes the role of mum and on it goes.

Little Tommy Tiddlemouse
This is similar to the game above. One player stands with back to the group which chants,

> Little Tommy Tiddlemouse
> Lives in a little house.
> Someone came knocking
> Oh me, oh my!
> Someone is saying
> It is I.

One child from the group speaks the last line alone and the first player has to identify who it is.

Mime
One player mimes an action and the others guess what it is.

Feely bag
Conceal an object in a pillow case and invite the children to guess what it is by touch alone.

Kim's game
A tray has five articles on it. Remove one of the articles without the children seeing which one. They have to guess which is missing from the tray.

Changes

This is another version of Kim's game. The adult helps to change the appearance of one child, e.g. adding a necklace or putting a jumper on back to front. The rest of the group has to guess what has changed.

Crocodile, Crocodile

Players stand in a line facing the 'crocodile' with a gap making an imaginary river. They chant 'Crocodile, crocodile may I cross your river?' The crocodile replies, 'Only if you're wearing something red' (for example).

Row, row, row the boat

Children, in pairs, sit facing each other and holding hands to form a boat shape. They then row backwards and forwards to the song,

> Row, row, row the boat
> Gently down the stream.
> Merrily, merrily, merrily, merrily,
> Life is but a dream.

The above are very common in many early years settings and we include them here not because we think they are novel but as a reminder that they are important. A good idea is to make an enlarged text of those games with a refrain, so that you have a ready-made source of ideas on the spot. You will also then have a set of texts which the children know well and which can be used in shared writing and reading activities.

8.4 Playing with language in the environment

Role play

Children will give roles to toys without any prompts. They will provide voices and actions for imaginary personalities as they play alone or together. 'Small world' toys are particularly successful in encouraging this kind of role play. Farm animals, toy cars and garages, dolls' houses and figures and lego people demand plot and character. The natural extension to this is to take on the character and this usually centres around the home corner or imaginative play area. Here are some suggestions for the imaginary play area which have literacy as a key focus.

A newspaper shop

We have already introduced this idea in the chapter on writing. The majority of the resources necessary for creating a newsagents are readily available from the families of the children: newspapers, magazines, comics, manuals, greetings cards, invitations, wrapping paper and gift tags, confectionery wrappings and boxes, videos, posters, order books, till and receipts. A visit to a local newsagents will give you an idea of the things to include in your shop and the children themselves can make many of the above items.

An office

The one we have seen was the office of a travel agent and contained travel brochures, flight tickets and plane seating plans for different aircraft, telephone and pad, booking forms/books, foreign money, atlas and maps, posters of other countries, typewriter, till, special offers, information texts relating to countries of the world, an entertainment desk with shows, operas, etc. Again, the stock of paperwork was added to from the children's own productions. They made flight tickets and posters advertising their local area.

A library

This was created following an actual visit to the local library and included books organised according to themes indicated by symbols designed by the children, an 'in' and 'out' desk with signs, library tickets, a children's/teddies' section with lists of recommended texts, a telephone, pamphlets of local attractions, instructions for how to find books, opening times, a tape section with playback facilities, a display of book jackets and posters from publishers, introductions to favourite authors and their work.

The possibilities are endless and these are just three we have seen and which the children have enjoyed. Another way to stimulate role play, using limited space and resources, is through the use of artefacts and dressing-up clothes. For example:

a coronet: princes and princesses
a suitcase: holidays
a gold coin: treasure
an umbrella: a rainy day
a large key: giants and castles
a fireman's helmet: fires and rescues
a broken toy: workshop.

The children will find ways of adding to these resources from the environment and from their imaginations. Children's imaginations are the vital resource and often the only resource needed both to stimulate and sustain role play. However, it will come as no surprise to you that we find some of the most effective stimuli for role play come from the books we use.

Texts are an excellent starting point for role play; they can be used to explore experience, feelings and relationships. They can be used to introduce new concepts and, through exploration of the themes and events of the text, children can gain a deeper understanding of the text. Literacy teachers need to know about children's books.

8.5 Planning, assessing, recording and reporting in play

In other chapters we have discussed the principles of planning, the role of observation and sampling and the purposes of assessment in relation to children's learning and informing those who are interested in the progress of the child. It is time to restate that planning, assessment, recording and reporting are part of a continuous ever developing cycle. We can best do this through the use of Figure 8.1.

From this you will see that the process of planning, activity and evaluation are continuous. You will also see that opportunities for the individual assessment of the child's achievements are thought about as part of the process and not as a 'bolt-on extra'. Whatever form of record-keeping you choose it should contain evidence of what has gone on in the setting and what the children, as groups and as individuals, learned from it. For the most part, evidence of the activity of the setting will be contained in the plans and evidence of the children's progress will appear in a profile of annotated and dated observation notes and samples. Each will inform the other, however, and both should inform interested parties and future plans.

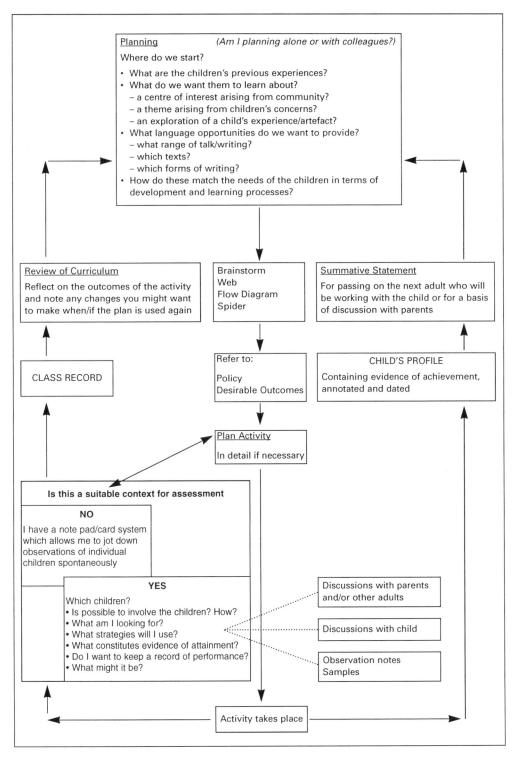

Figure 8.1 Assessment cycle

Teaching language and literacy in the early years is an exciting, fulfilling and rewarding task, yet it is also demanding and exacting. We began this book by reminding you that the context in which we write is one in which terms such as 'raising standards', 'setting targets' and 'explicit teaching' are the current terminology. It is important that children are encouraged to reach their full potential and to strive continually to extend and develop their understanding, knowledge and skills. It is important that as early years teachers we do not underestimate what very young children can do – they will often surprise us. It is essential, however, that we help to maintain children's love of learning and we can do this best by creating contexts and opportunities which exploit their natural curiosity and joy of life. We hope that we have helped you to do this within a firm understanding of why these things are important. We close by reminding you to keep playing, keep talking, keep writing and keep reading – for then you will be able to inspire the children in your care to do likewise.

Bibliography

Adams, M.J. (1990) *Beginning to Read: The New Phonics in Context*. Oxford: Heinemann.

Allen, D. (1987) *English, Whose English?* Sheffield: NATE

Association of assessment Inspectors and Advisers (1997) *Baseline assessment*. AAIA Publications.

Baddeley, B. (ed.) (1992) *Learning Together Through Talk*. London: Hodder and Stoughton.

Bain, R. (1991) *Reflections: Talking about Language*. London: Hodder and Stoughton.

Barrs, M., *et al.* (1988) *The Primary Language Record Handbook for Teachers*. London: Centre for Language in Primary Education.

Barrs, *et al.* (1990) *Patterns of Learning*. London: Centre for Language in Primary Education.

Barrs, M. and Thomas, A. (eds) (1991) *The Reading Book*. London: Centre for Language in Primary Education.

Bennett, N and Kell, J. (1989) *A Good Start? Four Year Olds in Infant Schools*. Oxford: Basil Blackwell.

Brindley, S. (ed.) (1994) *Teaching English*. London: Routledge.

Bromley, H. (1996) 'What's that dog thinking, Mrs Bromley?: Picture Books and Learning to Read.' in Whitebread, D. (ed) *Teaching and Learning in the Early Years*. London: Routledge.

Bryant, P. and Bradley, L. (1985) *Children's Reading Problems*. Oxford: Blackwell.

Buckley, J., James, F., Kerr, A. (1996) *Rhyme: A Resource for Teachers of Reading*. Suffolk County Council.

Butler, D. (1979) *Cushla and her Books*. London: Hodder and Stoughton.

Cambourne, B. (1997) Paper presented at UKRA conference, University of Manchester.

Campbell, R. (1996) *Literacy in Nursery Education*. Stoke-on-Trent: Trentham Books.

Carter, R. (ed) (1991) *Knowledge About Language*. London: Hodder and Stoughton.

Chomsky, N. (1968) *Language and Mind*. New York: Harcourt Brace Jovanovich.

Chukovsky, K. (1963) *From Two to Five*. Berkeley: University of California Press.

Clay, M.M. (1975) *What Did I Write?* Auckland, N.Z.: Heinemann.

Cripps, C. (1992) *Joining the ABC*. London: Language Development Aids.

Czerniewska, P. (1989a) *The National Writing Project: Becoming a Writer*. Surrey: Thomas Nelson and Sons.

Czerniewska, P. (1989b) *The National Writing Project: Responding to and Assessing Writing*. Surrey: Thomas Nelson and Sons.

DES (1989) *English for Ages 5 to 16*. London: HMSO.

DfEE (1996) *The Next Steps*. London: DfEE.

Dombey, H. (1992) *Words and Worlds: Reading in the Early Years of School*. National Association of Advisers in English.

Donaldson, M. (1978) *Children's Minds*. Glasgow: William Collins.

Ferreiro, E. and Teberosky, A. (1983) *Literacy Before Schooling*. London: Heinemann.

Fox, C. (1993) *At the Very Edge of the Forest*. London: Cassell.

Freud, S. (1923) *The Standard Edition of the Complete Psychological Works of Sigmund Freud*. London: Hogarth Press.

Goodman, K. and Goodman, Y. (1979) 'Learning to read is natural.' in Resnick, L. and

Weaver, P. (eds) *Theory and Practice of Early Reading*. Hillsdale, NJ: Lawrence Erlbaum.

Goodman, Y. M. (1985) 'Kidwatching: Observing Children in the Classroom', in Jaggar, A. and Smith-Burke, M.T. (eds) *Observing the Language User*. Newark: International Reading Association.

Goodman, Y. (1990) 'The Development of Initial Literacy', in Carter, R. (ed.) *Knowledge about Language and the Curriculum*. London: Hodder & Stoughton.

Goswami, U. and Bryant, P. (1991) *Phonological Skills and Learning to Read*. Hillsdale, NJ: Lawrence Erlbaum.

Goswami, U. (1994) 'Reading by Analogy', in Hilme, C. and Snowling, M. (eds) *Reading Development and Dyslexia*. London: Whurr Publishers.

Goswami, U. (1995) 'Rhyme in Children's Early Reading.' in Beard, R. (ed.) *Rhyme, Reading and Writing*. London: Hodder and Stoughton.

Gough, P. (1972) 'One Second of Reading.' in Kavanagh, J. and Mattingley, I. (eds) *Language by Ear and Eye*. Cambridge, Mass.: MIT Press.

Graham, J. and Kelly, A. (1997) *Reading Under Control: Teaching Reading in the Primary School*. London: David Fulton Publishers.

Groos, K. (1901) *The Play of Man*. London: Heinemann.

Hall, G. S. (1908) *Adolescence*. New York: Appleton.

Hall, N. (1987) *The Emergence of Literacy*. Sevenoaks: Edward Arnold.

Hardy, B. (1975) *Tellers and Listeners*. Athlone Press.

Harste, J., Woodward, V., Burke, C. (1984) *Language Stories and Literacy Lessons*. Portsmouth, NH: Heinemann Educational Books.

Heath, S. B. (1983) *Ways With Words*. Cambridge: Cambridge University Press.

Hendy, L. (1995) *Playing, Role-Playing and Dramatic Activity in Early Years*. Vol 15, No 2. Stoke-on-Trent: Trentham Books.

Hester, H. (1993) *Guide to the Primary Learning Record*. London: Centre for Language in Primary Education.

Hohmann, M., Banet, B., Weikart, D. (1979) *Young Children in Action*. Ypsilanti, Mich.: High Scope Press.

Holdaway, D. (1979) *The Foundations of Literacy*. Sydney: Ashton Scholastic.

Howe, A. and Johnson, J. (1992) *Common Bonds: Storytelling in the Classroom*. London: Hodder and Stoughton.

Hutt, C. (1989) 'Fantasy Play', in Hutt, S.J. *et al.* (eds) *Play, Exploration and Learning*. London: Routledge.

Ingram, J. (1993) *Talk, Talk, Talk*. London: Penguin Books.

Isaacs, S. (1929) *The Nursery Years*. London: Routledge and Kegan Paul.

Karavais, S. and Davies, P. (1995) *Progress in English: Assessment and Record Keeping at KS1 and 2*. Reading and Language Information Centre: University of Reading.

Language in the National Curriculum (LINC) (1992) *Materials for Professional Development*. Unpublished.

Lightfoot, M. and Martin, N. (1988) *The Word for Teaching is Learning*. Oxford: Heinemann Education.

Meadows, S. (1992) *Understanding Child Development*. London: Routledge.

Meek, M., Warlow, A., Barton, G. (1978) *The Cool Web: The Pattern of Children's Learning*. London: The Bodley Head.

Meek, M. (1987) *Learning to Read*. London: The Bodley Head.

Meek, M. (1988) *How Texts Teach What Readers Learn*. Stroud: Thimble Press.

Meek, M. (1991) *On Being Literate*. London: Bodley Head.

Mittens, B. (1987) *English: Not the Naming of Parts*. Sheffield: NATE.

National Centre for Literacy (1997) *The National Literacy Project Framework for Teaching*. Reading: National Literacy Centre.

Norman, K. (ed.) (1992) *Thinking Voices*. London: Hodder & Stoughton.

OFSTED (1996) *The Teaching of Reading in 45 Inner London Primary Schools*. London: OFSTED

Open University (1981) *Curriculum in Action: an approach to Evaluation. P234*. Milton Keynes: Open University Press.

Opie, I. and P. (1959) *The Lore and Language of Schoolchildren*. Oxford: Oxford University Press.

Paley, V.B. (1981) *Wally's Stories*. London: Harvard University Press.

Peters, M. L. (1985) *Spelling: Caught or Taught?* London: Routledge and Kegan Paul.

Pigat, J. (1951) *Play, Dreams and Imitation in Childhood*. London: Routledge and Kegan Paul.

Reid, J., Forrestal, P., Cook, J. (1989) *Small Group Learning in the Classroom*. Perth: Chalkface Press.

Richmond, J. And Savva, H. (1990) *NLLC Planning and Assessment Framework*. North London Language Consortium. Anderson Fraser.

Rosen, B. (1988) *And none Of It Was Nonsense*. London: Mary Glasgow Publications.

Sassoon, R. (1990) *Handwriting: A New Perspective*. Cheltenham: Stamley Thornes Publishers.

SCAA (1996) *Desirable Outcomes for Children's Learning on Entering Compulsory Education*. London: DfEE

Smith, F. (1978) *Reading*. Cambridge: Cambridge University Press.

Smith, F. (1982) *Writing and the Writer*. London: Heinemann Educational.

Smith. P. K. and Cowie, H. (1988) *Understanding Children's Development*. Oxford: Basil Blackwell.

Southgate, V. and Arnold, H. (1981) *Extending Beginning Reading*. London: Heinemann for the School Council.

Spencer, S. H. (1878) *The Principles of Psychology*. New York: Appleton.

Stanovich, K. (1980) 'Towards an interactive-compensatory model of individual differences in the development of reaading.' *Reading Research Quarterly*. **1**, 32–71.

Stierer, B. *et al.* (1993) *Profiling, Recording and Observing*. London: Routledge.

Sylva, K. (1977) 'Play and Learning' in Tizard, B. and Harvey, D. (eds) *The Biology of Play*. London: Heinemann.

Tann, S. (1991) *Developing Language in the Primary Classroom*. London: Cassell.

Temple, C., *et al.* (1988) *The Beginnings of Writing*. Boston, Mas.: Allyn and Bacon.

Tizard, B. and Hughes, M. (1984) *Young Children Learning: Talking and Thinking at Home and at School*. London: Fontana Paperbacks.

Torbe, M. (1977) *Teaching Spelling*. Sussex: Ward Lock Educational.

Vygotsky, L. (1962) *Thought and Language*. Cambridge, Mass.: MIT Press.

Wade, B. and Moore, M. (1996) 'Home activities: the advent of literacy. *European Early Childhood Education Research Journal*. **4** (2) 63–76.

Weinberger, J., Hannon, P., Nutbrown, C. (1990) *Ways of Working with Parents to Promote Early Literacy Development*, Sheffield: University of Sheffield.

Wells, G. (1987) *The Meaning Makers: Children Learning Language and Using Language to Learn*. London: Hodder & Stoughton.

Wendon, L. (1986) *First Steps in Letterland*. Barton: Letterland.

Wilkinson, A. (1965) *Spoken English*. University of Birmingham School of Education.

Wray, D. and Medwell, J. (1991) *Language and Literacy in the Primary Years*. London: Routledge.

Wray, D. and Medwell, J. (1994) *Teaching Primary English: The State of the Art*. London: Routledge.

Children's books

Ahlberg, A. and J. (1978) *Each Peach Pear Plum*. London: Kestrel/Viking.

Armitage, R. and D. *The Lighthousekeeper's Lunch*. New Zealand: Scholastic.

Blake, Q. *Mr. Magnolia*. London: Collins Picture Lions.

Briggs, R. *The Snowman*. London: Random House.

Burningham, J. (1973) *Mr. Gumpy's Outing*. Picture Puffin.

Burningham, J. (1984) *Granpa*. London: Jonathan Cape.

Campbell, R. *Dear Zoo*. London: Picture Puffin.

Cambridge Reading (1996) Cambridge: Cambridge University Press.

Grindley, S. *Knock Knock Who's There?* London: Magnet.

Hayes, S. (1986) *This is the Bear*. London: Walker Books.

Hawkins, C. and J. (1984) *Mig the Pig*. Picture Puffins.

Hughes, S. (1981) *Alfie Gets in First*. London: Fontana Picture Lions.

Hutchins, P. (1969) *Rosie's Walk*. London: Bodley Head.

Hutchins, P. (1972) *Titch*. London: Bodley Head.

Hutchins, P. (1983) *You'll Soon Grow into Them, Titch*. London: Bodley Head.

Hutchins, P. (1969) *The Doorbell Rang*. London: Bodley Head.

Inkpen, M. *Kipper*. London: Bodley Head.

McDonald, M. and Pritchatt, S. (1978) *Lucy says No*. Dinosaur.

McKee, D. (1980) *Not Now, Bernard*. London: Anderson Press.

Murphy, J. (1980) *Peace at Last*. London: Walker Books.

Nicholl, H. (1972) *Meg and Mog*. London: Heinemann.

Ormerod, J. (1981) *Sunshine*. London: Picture Puffin.

Rosen, M. and Oxenbury, H. (1989) *We're Going on a Bearhunt*. London: Walker Books.

Sendak, M. (1963) *Where The Wild Things Are*. London: Bodley Head.

Sendak, M. (1963) *Hector Protector and As I Went Oer the Water*. London: Bodley Head.

Seuss, Dr. (1957) *The Cat in the Hat Comes Back*. New York: Random House.

Sowter, N. (1977) *Maisie Middleton*. London: Collins Picture Lions.

Waddell, M. and Firth, B. (1988) *Can't You Sleep, Little Bear?* London: Walker Books.

Index